33

table of contents

so much to do, so little time—you're always on the go! You'd relish a moment to do something relaxing and enjoyable, like crochet. Easy! All you need is a small, portable project—the kind you can tote to kids' activities, family gatherings, and appointments—one that's so easy you can pull it out, work a few rows or rounds, and then set it aside without losing a beat. And that's just what you'll find in this collection: quick, fun-to-crochet designs for your home and family, plus information to reacquaint you with stitches and abbreviations and guide you to projects that suit (or stretch) your skills. So get going, and have a happy crochet!

gracious gifts

Think you need a special occasion for gift-giving? With designs as sweet and quick to crochet as these, you can make them up to give out "just because."

a rosy posy

Could a rose by any other name hold a place as sweetly? This single blossom is the perfect alternative to folding down page corners.

ROSE BOOKMARK

SKILL LEVEL

Easy

SIZE

finished measurement

14" long after felting

SHOP

yarns

Classic Merino Wool from Patons (Art. 244077)
100% wool; 3½ oz. (100 g); 223 yds. (204 m); worsted weight

- 1 ball #209 Old Rose (A)
- 1 ball #240 Leaf Green (B)

4 MEDIUM

hook & extra

- Size J/10 (6 mm) crochet hook OR SIZE NEEDED TO OBTAIN GAUGE
- Blunt-end yarn needle

PREP

gauge

14 sc and 14 rows = 4" (10 cm). TAKE TIME TO CHECK YOUR GAUGE.

CROCHET

ROSE

With A, ch 3.

Rnd 1: Work 8 dc in 3rd ch from hook, join with sl st to top of beg ch-3—9 dc, counting beg ch-3 as dc.

Rnd 2: *Ch 6, sk next dc, sl st in next dc; rep from * 3 more times.

Rnd 3: Rep Rnd 2, working sl sts in skipped sts from Rnd 2.

Rnd 4: *Ch 6, sl st around vertical post of next dc on Rnd 1 by passing hook under post; rep from * around.

Rnd 5: *Ch 4, sl st around vertical post of next dc on Rnd 1 by passing hook under post; rep from * around; fasten off. Weave in ends.

LEAF (make 2)

With B, ch 3.

Row 1: 4 dc in 3rd ch from hook; turn.

Row 2: Ch 3—counts as dc; sk first dc, dc in each of next 3 dc; turn.

Row 3: Ch 3, sk first dc, (yo and draw up a lp in next dc, yo and draw through 2 lps on hook) 2 times, yo and draw up lp in top of ch-3; yo and draw through all lps on hook, ch 1, and fasten off. Weave in ends.

STEM

With B, ch for 14". Fasten off and weave in ends.

FELTING

See page 7 for felting instructions.

FINISHING

Sew the Leaves and the Rose to the Stem.

Design by Linda Cyr

sitting pretty

Yesterday's biggest mistake is today's hottest craze. Crochet these table accents with wool, throw them in the washing machine, and you'll have felted masterpieces.

STRIPED BOWL

SKILL LEVEL

Easy

SIZE

finished measurements

17" diameter before felting; 10" diameter after felting

SHOP

yarns

Classic Merino Wool from Patons (Art. 244077)
100% wool; 3½ oz. (100 g); 223 yds. (204 m); worsted weight

- 2 balls #203 Maize (A)
- 1 ball #240 Leaf Green (B)

4 MEDIUM

hook & extra

- Size H/8 (5 mm) crochet hook OR SIZE NEEDED TO OBTAIN GAUGE
- Blunt-end yarn needle

PREP

gauge

16 hdc and 12 rows = 4" (10 cm). TAKE TIME TO CHECK YOUR GAUGE.

CROCHET

Beg at base, with A, ch 3.

Rnd 1: Work 9 hdc in 3rd ch from hook; join with sl st in top of ch-2—10 hdc.

Rnd 2: Ch 2—counts as hdc; hdc in same sp, 2 hdc in each hdc around; join with sl st in top of ch-2—20 hdc.

Rnd 3: Ch 2, (2 hdc in next hdc, hdc in next hdc) 9 times, 2 hdc in next hdc; join—30 hdc.

Rnd 4: Ch 2, (2 hdc in next hdc, hdc in each of next 2 hdc) 9 times, 2 hdc in next hdc, hdc in next hdc; join—40 hdc.

Rnds 5–14: Cont to inc 10 sts evenly around on each rnd as est—140 hdc at end of Rnd 14.

Rnds 15–26: Ch 2, hdc in each hdc around.

Rnd 27: With B, ch 2, hdc in each hdc around; join A.

Rnds 28–29: With A, ch 2, hdc in each hdc around; join B at end of Rnd 29.

Rnd 30: Rep Rnd 27.

Rnd 31: With A, ch 2, hdc in each hdc around; join.

Rnd 32: Ch 2, (hdc in each of next 12 hdc, sk next hdc, hdc in next hdc) 10 times, ending last rep with sl st in top of ch 2—130 hdc.

Rnd 33: Ch 2, (hdc in each of next 11 hdc, sk next hdc, hdc in next hdc) 10 times, ending last rep with sl st in top of ch-2—120 hdc.

Rnd 34: Ch 2, (hdc in each of next 10 hdc, sk next hdc, hdc in next hdc) 10 times, ending last rep with sl st in top of ch-2—110 hdc. Fasten off. Weave in all ends.

FELTING

See page 7 for felting instructions.

Design by Jane Davis

PLAID TABLE RUNNER

SKILL LEVEL

Easy

SIZE

finished measurements

13×59" before felting; 10½×59" after felting

SHOP

yarns

Classic Merino Wool from Patons (Art. 244077)
100% wool; 3½ oz. (100 g); 223 yds. (204 m); worsted weight

- 2 balls #238 Paprika (A)
- 1 ball #231 Chestnut Brown (B)
- 1 ball #203 Maize (C)
- 1 ball #204 Old Gold (D)
- 1 ball #77707 That's Red (E)
- 1 ball #240 Leaf Green (F)

4 MEDIUM

hooks & extra

- Size H/8 (5 mm) crochet hook OR SIZE NEEDED TO OBTAIN GAUGE
- Size G/6 (4 mm) crochet hook
- Size F/5 (3.75 mm) crochet hook
- Blunt-end yarn needle

PREP

gauge

17 sc and 20 rows = 4" (10 cm) with largest hook. TAKE TIME TO CHECK YOUR GAUGE.

CROCHET

With largest hook and A, ch 47.

Row 1: Sc in 2nd ch from hook and each ch across—46 sc; turn.

Row 2: Ch 1, sc in each sc across; turn.

With A, rep last row of sc 14 more times. *With B, work 2 rows; with C, work 6 rows; with F, work 2 rows; with D, work 16 rows; with E, work 2 rows; with C, work 6 rows; with B, work 2 rows; with A, work 16 rows; rep from * 4 more times; fasten off.

Chain-Stitch Embroidery

With largest hook, join E at center of bottom edge. Work a raised running chain up center st of Runner by working one ch st over each row of sc, holding yarn at back of work. Rep with F on 11th st to right of center st and with B on 3rd st from F st; rep with B on 11th st to left of center st and with F on 3rd st from B st.

Border

Rnd 1: With largest hook, join B with sl st in center of one side of Runner and work 1 rnd of sc evenly around, working 3 sc in each corner; join with sl st to first sc.

Rnd 2: With next smallest hook, ch 1, sc in each sc around, working 3 sc in each corner sc; join with sl st to first sc.

Rnds 3–4: With F, rep Rnd 2.

Rnds 5–6: With smallest hook and B, rep Rnd 2; fasten off. Weave in ends.

FELTING

See page 7 for felting instructions.

Design by Jane Davis

cool tools for crafters

This useful set—crocheted in wool and then machine-washed to felt—is a thoughtful idea for surprising your best crafting pals.

CROCHET HOOK CADDY

SKILL LEVEL

Easy

SIZE

finished measurements

4½" tall and 2½" in diameter after felting

SHOP

yarns

Classic Merino Wool from Patons (Art. 244077)
100% wool; 3½ oz. (100 g); 223 yds. (204 m); worsted weight

- 1 ball #208 Burgundy (A)
- 1 ball #209 Old Rose (B)
- 1 ball #240 Leaf Green (C)

4 MEDIUM

hook & extras

- Size J/10 (6 mm) crochet hook OR SIZE NEEDED TO OBTAIN GAUGE
- Plastic liner: 4½" tall with a 2½" diameter (sample uses an 8-quart sugar-free drink mix container)
- Blunt-end yarn needle

PREP

gauge

14 sc and 14 rows = 4" (10 cm). TAKE TIME TO CHECK YOUR GAUGE.

CROCHET

Beg at base, with A, ch 2.

Rnd 1: Work 6 sc in 2nd ch from hook, place marker to mark beg of rnd.

Rnds 2–3: Work 2 sc in each sc around—24 sc at end of Rnd 3.

Rnd 4: Sc in each sc around.

Rnd 5: *Sc in next sc, 2 sc in next sc; rep from * around—36 sc.

Beg sides, work rnds of sc as foll, carrying unused colors loosely on the inside: 2 B, 1 C, 2 A, 2 B, 2 C, 1 A, 1 B, 2 C, 2 A, 2 B, 1 C, 2 A. Fasten off; weave in ends.

FELTING

See instructions at right.

Design by Linda Cyr

FLOWER PINCUSHION

SKILL LEVEL

Easy

SIZE

finished measurement

4½" diameter after felting

SHOP

yarns

Classic Merino Wool from Patons (Art. 244077)
100% wool; 3½ oz. (100 g); 223 yds. (204 m); worsted weight

- 1 ball #208 Burgundy (A)
- 1 ball #204 Old Gold (B)

4 MEDIUM

hook & extras

- Size J/10 (6 mm) crochet hook OR SIZE NEEDED TO OBTAIN GAUGE
- Polyester fiberfill
- Blunt-end yarn needle

PREP

gauge

14 sc and 14 rows = 4" (10 cm). TAKE TIME TO CHECK YOUR GAUGE.

CROCHET

CENTER (make 2: 1 with A; 1 with B)

Ch 2.

Rnd 1: Work 6 sc in 2nd ch from hook, place marker to mark beg of rnd.

Rnds 2–3: Work 2 sc in each sc around—12 sc.

Rnd 4: Sc in each sc around.

Rnd 5: *Sc in next sc, 2 sc in next sc; rep from * around—36 sc; fasten off B Center. Do not fasten off A Center.

PETALS

Place B Center on top of A Center, lining up sts. With A, join the 2 center edges with a rnd of sc worked through both thicknesses, stuffing with fiberfill before completing rnd—36 sts around.

Next rnd: *Sk next st, 5 dc in next st, sk next st, sl st in next st; rep from * around—9 Petals; fasten off. Weave in all ends.

FELTING

See instructions at right.

Design by Linda Cyr

FELTING

Place piece(s) in a mesh lingerie bag and put in washing machine with a small amount of mild soap (avoid detergent), along with other lint-free items such as old jeans or T-shirts (which provide necessary agitation to promote felting). Use a hot-wash cycle and cold rinse. Check piece(s) every few minutes to ensure felting is successful—the stitches should visually disappear. If you remove the item(s) in the middle of the wash cycle, hand-rinse in cold water and roll in a towel to remove excess water. Shape damp felted piece(s) to measurements and dry flat. Do not put felted piece(s) in the dryer.

Note: For the Striped Bowl shown on *page 4*, shape the damp felted piece over a bowl of similar size and let dry.

stash & go carryalls

With the waist-wise mini at *left* and a zippered bag, *opposite*—bagging your essentials has never been more fun!

MINI FANNY PACK

SKILL LEVEL

Beginner

SIZE

finished measurements

9×5"

SHOP

yarns

Lion Cotton from Lion Brand (Art. 760)
100% cotton; 5 oz. (140 g); 236 yds. (212 m); worsted weight

- 1 ball #108 Morning Glory Blue (A)
- 1 ball #146 Fuchsia (B)

4 MEDIUM

hook & extras

- Size H/8 (5 mm) crochet hook OR SIZE NEEDED TO OBTAIN GAUGE
- Two ⅝"-diameter buttons
- Fabric for lining
- Sewing thread to match lining
- Sewing needle
- Blunt-end yarn needle

PREP

gauge

16 sc and 16 rows = 4" (10 cm). TAKE TIME TO CHECK YOUR GAUGE.

CROCHET

MAIN PIECE

With A, ch 35.

Row 1 (RS): Sc in 2nd ch from hook and sc in each ch across; turn—34 sc.

Row 2: Ch 1, sc in each sc across; turn.

Rep last row until work measures 10½"; fasten off.

GUSSET (make 2)

With B, ch 8.

Work in sc over 7 sc as for Main Piece until work measures 4½"; fasten off.

BELT CASING AND FLAP

With B, ch 35 and work in sc over 34 sc until piece measures 2" (Belt Casing), ending with a WS row.

Join to Main Piece

Next row (RS): Ch 1, place row just worked on top of final row of Main Piece; work 1 row of sc through both pieces to join; turn.

Cont with B in sc for 1½" more (Flap).

Buttonhole row: Ch 1, sc in each of next 6 sc, ch 2, sk next 2 sc, sc in each of next 18 sc, ch 2, sk next 2 sc, sc in each of last 6 sc; turn.

Next row: Ch 1, sc in each of first 6 sc, 2 sc in next ch-2 sp, sc in each of next 18 sc, 2 sc in next ch-2 sp, sc in each of last 6 sc; turn. Work 3 more rows sc; fasten off.

FINISHING

Using Main Piece as a guide, cut fabric lining to same measurement adding a ½" seam allowance. With B, slip-stitch Gussets to sides of Main Piece. With B, work one row of sc around edge of Flap, working 3 sc in corners. Press seam allowance to WS of fabric lining; sew to inside of Main Piece using needle and thread. Sew on buttons. Sew foundation row of Casing in position on back of Main Piece. Slide Belt in place through Casing.

Design by Veronica Manno

ZIPPERED BAG

SKILL LEVEL

■□□□ **Beginner**

SIZE

finished measurements

3½×4½"

SHOP

yarns

Sugar'n Cream from Lily (Art. 102001)

100% cotton; 2½ oz. (71½ g); 120 yds. (110 m); worsted weight

- 1 ball #1317 Hot Purple (A)
- 1 ball #2 Black (B)

4 MEDIUM

hook & extras

- Size H/8 (5 mm) crochet hook OR SIZE NEEDED TO OBTAIN GAUGE
- Small safety pin for marker
- 5" matching zipper
- Small felt shapes, buttons, or beads for decorations
- Sewing needle and thread
- Blunt-end yarn needle

PREP

gauge

14 sts and 16 rnds = 4" (10 cm) in sc. TAKE TIME TO CHECK YOUR GAUGE.

CROCHET

With A, ch 17.

Rnd 1 (RS): Work 2 sc in 2nd ch from hook, sc in next 14 ch, work 3 sc in last ch, do not turn; working along the opposite side of the ch, sc in next 14 ch, sc in same ch as first sc, do not join, mark last st made with safety pin—34 sts. You will now be working in a spiral, marking the last st made with the safety pin to indicate end of rnd.

Rnds 2–8: Sc in each st around.

Rnd 9: Sc in each st around, join rnd with a sl st in first st, removing safety pin. Fasten off. With RS facing, join B with a sc in side edge opposite joining of Rnd 9.

Rnd 10: Sc in each st around, do not join, mark last st made with safety pin. You will now be working in a spiral, marking the last st made with the safety pin to indicate end of rnd.

Rnds 11–13: Sc in each st around.

Rnd 14: Sc in each st around, join rnd with a sl st in first st; remove safety pin; fasten off.

FINISHING

Trim zipper to fit. Sew in zipper using backstitches and matching thread.

LOOP

With A, and leaving a long tail, ch 17.

Row 1: Sl st in 2nd ch from hook and in each ch across, then sl st in first st to form a loop; fasten off, leaving a long tail.

Thread one tail into yarn needle. Insert needle into upper corner of Bag, drawing end through to WS. Rep for other tail, inserting yarn needle one st away. Tie tail ends tog in a firm knot on WS of Bag. Sew on decorations as desired.

Design by Veronica Manno

make a splash!

Welcome friends and relatives to your guest room with their very own handmade facecloth and bath mitt.

FACECLOTH

SKILL LEVEL

Easy

SIZE

finished measurements

12×12"

SHOP

yarn

Sugar'n Cream Solid from Lily (Art. 102001)

100% cotton; 2½ oz. (70 g); 120 yds. (109 m); worsted weight

- 1 ball #10 Yellow OR
- 1 ball #07 Ivory

hook & extra

- Size H/8 (3.75 mm) crochet hook OR SIZE NEEDED TO OBTAIN GAUGE
- Blunt-end yarn needle

PREP

gauge

18 sts and 18 rows = 4" (10 cm). TAKE TIME TO CHECK YOUR GAUGE.

CROCHET

Ch 50.

Row 1 (RS): Sc in 2nd ch from hook, *ch 1, sk next ch, sc in next ch; rep from * across—25 sc with ch-1 bet; turn.

Row 2: Ch 1, sc in first st, *ch 1, sk next st, sc in each of next 2 sts, ch 1, sk next st, sc in next st; rep from * to last 3 sts, ch 1, sk next st, sc in each of last 2 sts; turn.

Row 3: Ch 1, sc in first st, *ch 1, sk next st, sc in next st; rep from * across; turn.

Rep Rows 2–3 for pat until work measures 12". Do not fasten off; cont as foll for edging:

Edging

Rnd 1: With RS facing, join yarn with sl st in any corner and work 1 rnd of sc evenly around outer edge, working 3 sc in corners; join with sl st to first sc.

Rnd 2: Ch 1, sc in same sp as last sl st, *sk next sc, 4 hdc in next sc, sk next sc, sc in next sc; rep from * around; join with sl st to first sc. Fasten off. Weave in ends.

BATH MITT

SKILL LEVEL

Easy

SIZE

finished measurement

9½" high

SHOP

yarns

Sugar'n Cream Ombre from Lily (Art. 102002)

100% cotton; 2 oz. (56 g); 95 yds. (86 m); worsted weight

- 1 ball #02713 Key Lime Pie (MC) OR
- 1 ball #02605 Creamsicle (MC)

Sugar'n Cream Solid from Lily (Art. 102001)

100% cotton; 2½ oz. (70 g); 120 yds. (109 m); worsted weight

- 1 ball #10 Yellow (A) OR
- 1 ball #07 Ivory (A)

hook & extra

- Size H/8 (3.75 mm) crochet hook OR SIZE NEEDED TO OBTAIN GAUGE
- Blunt-end yarn needle

PREP

gauge

18 sts and 18 rows = 4" (10 cm). TAKE TIME TO CHECK YOUR GAUGE.

special abbreviation

Sc2tog = Draw up a loop in each of next 2 stitches, yarn over and draw through all loops on hook.

CROCHET

With MC, ch 20.

Row 1: Sc in 2nd ch from hook and each ch across—19 sc; turn.

Row 2: Ch 1, sc in first st, *ch 1, sk next st, sc in next st; rep from * across; turn.

Row 3: Ch 1, sc in first st, *ch 1, sk next st, sc in each of next 2 sts, ch 1, sk next st, sc in next st; rep from * to last 3 sts, ch 1, sk next st, sc in each of last 2 sts; turn.

Row 4: Ch 1, sc in each st across, turn.

Rep Rows 2–4 for pat.

Shape Side

Keeping to pat, inc 1 st at beg of next row and every foll 4th row 3 more times—23 sts. Work 1 row even in pat.

Shape Thumb

Next row: Ch 1, work pat across first 7 sts, turn. Leave rem sts unworked.

Work 3 more rows in pat on these sts, and at the same time, inc 1 st at side edge on every row—10 sts.

Next row: Ch 1, sc2tog, pat to last 2 sts, sc2tog; turn.

Rep last row twice more—4 sts. Fasten off.

Sk next st after thumb, join MC to next st, ch 1, sc in same sp, work pat to end; turn.

Work one row even in pat.

Shape Side

Keeping to pat, inc one st at beg of next row and foll 6th row—17 sts. Work even in pat until work measures 8" from beg.

Next row: Ch 1, sc2tog, pat to last 2 sts, sc2tog; turn.

Rep last row once more—13 sts; fasten off.

FINISHING

Place two pieces tog and using A, beg at lower corner under thumb, work one rnd of sc around outer edges through both thicknesses to join and around lower opening of each piece separately.

Next rnd: Ch 1, working from left to right, work one reverse sc (see Crochet Basics for reverse single crochet instructions) in each sc around , ch 7 for hanging lp at end of rnd and join with sl st to first sc. Fasten off. Note that reverse sc is worked only on the top side (RS) of the wrist opening.

Designs by Ann Berry

afghans & pillows

Take your project outside, to your next appointment, even to a Saturday game—each of these comforts is super portable, so you can work on it almost anywhere.

stripe up the bands

If you love making blankets, you'll definitely want to add this cheerful design to your repertoire. Done in single crochet, its colors run in bands across the piece, then in rows around it to stripe the edging.

RAINBOW THROW

SKILL LEVEL

Easy

SIZE

finished measurements

30×40"

SHOP

yarns

Baby Coordinates from Bernat (Art. 166009)
75.2% acrylic, 22.2% acetate, 2.6% nylon; 6 oz. (170 g); 471 yds. (430 m); lightweight

3 LIGHT

- 1 ball #09412 Sweet Pink (A)
- 1 ball #01013 Soft Turquoise (B)
- 1 ball #09612 Daisy Yellow (C)
- 1 ball #09131 Blue Bon Bon (D)

hook & extra

- Size J/10 (6 mm) crochet hook OR SIZE NEEDED TO OBTAIN GAUGE
- Blunt-end yarn needle

PREP

gauge

16 sts and 18 rows = 4" (10 cm) in pat. TAKE TIME TO CHECK YOUR GAUGE.

CROCHET

With A, ch 121.

Foundation row: Sc in 2nd ch from hook, sc in next ch, *ch 1, sk ch, sc in next ch; rep from * across, turn—120 sts.

Row 1: Ch 1, sc in first sc, sc in next ch-1 sp, *ch 1, sk next sc, sc next ch-1 sp; rep from * to last 2 sc, ch 1, sk next sc, sc in last sc; turn.

Rows 2–3: Rep Row 1.

Rep Row 1 for pat in the foll color sequence: 8 rows B, 12 rows C, 16 rows D, 16 rows A, 12 rows B, 12 rows C, 16 rows D, 12 rows C, 12 rows B, 16 rows A, 16 rows D, 12 rows C, 8 rows B, 4 rows A. Do not fasten off.

Border

Rnd 1: With RS facing, cont with A and work 1 rnd of sc evenly around outer edge of throw, working 3 sc in each corner; join with sl st to first sc.

Rnd 2: Join B in center sc of any corner sc and work sc evenly around, working 3 sc in each corner sc; join with sl st to first sc.

Rnd 3: With C, rep Rnd 2.

Rnd 4: With D, rep Rnd 2.

Weave in all loose ends.

Design by Bobbi Anderson

mosaic inspiration

Draped over a sofa or chair, this striking 30-patch afghan invites you to sit down and curl up. Add a comfy pillow or two, and you're set for an afternoon of rest and relaxation.

MOSAIC COMFORTS

SKILL LEVEL

Experienced

SIZE

finished measurements

Throw = 37½×44"
Pillows = 14" square

SHOP

yarns

Lion Chenille from Lion Brand (Art. 530)
100% acrylic; 3 oz. (85 g);
174 yds. (158 m); worsted weight

4 MEDIUM

For throw

- 5 balls #125 Mocha (A)
- 5 balls #111 Denim Blue (B)

For pillow

- 2 balls #111 Denim Blue or #125 Mocha

hook & extras

- Size H/8 (5 mm) crochet hook OR SIZE NEEDED TO OBTAIN GAUGE
- Blunt-end yarn needle
- 14"-square form for each pillow

PREP

gauge

In Seed st, 14 sts and 14 rows = 4" (10 cm).
One mosaic square with edging = 6½" (16.5 cm).
TAKE TIME TO CHECK YOUR GAUGE.

Note: To change color in single crochet, work up to one stitch before next color, draw up loop in next stitch with color in use; with new color, complete the single crochet.

CROCHET

PATTERN STITCH

Seed Stitch (a multiple of 2 sts + 1; a rep of 2 rows)

Row 1 and all odd-numbered rows (WS): Ch 1, sc in first sc; *sc in next ch-1 sp, ch 1, sk next sc; rep from * across; end with sc in ch-1 sp, sc in last sc; turn.

Row 2 and all even-numbered rows (RS): Ch 1, sc in first sc; *ch 1, sk next sc, sc in next ch-1 sp; rep from * across; end with ch 1, sk sc, sc in last sc; turn.

Rep Rows 1 and 2 for Seed st pat.

THROW

SQUARE I (make 15)

With A, ch 22.

Foundation row (RS): Sc in 2nd ch from hook; *ch 1, sk next ch, sc in next ch; rep from * across—21 sts; turn. Work Row 1 of Seed st.

Row 2 (RS): Work Row 2 of Seed st pat and Row 1 of the chart, *below right.*

Row 3: Work Row 1 of Seed st pat and Row 2 of chart.

Rows 4–20: Cont in pat and work from the chart through Row 19; fasten off at end of Row 20.

Edging

Rnd 1: With RS facing, join B with sl st in first ch-1 sp near top right corner, ch 1, sc in same sp. (Ch 1, sk next sc, sc in next ch-1 sp) 8 times, ch 1, sk next sc, 3 sc in last ch-1 sp. (Ch 1, sk next row, sc in next row) 9 times down left side, ch 1, sk 1 row, 3 sc in next row. (Ch 1, sc in next ch-1 sp) 9 times along lower edge, ch 1, 3 sc in last ch-1 sp. (Ch 1, sk next row, sc in next row) 9 times up right side, ch 1, sk next row, 3 sc in next row, ch 1; join with sl st in first sc.

Rnd 2: In first ch-1 sp work sl st, ch 1, and sc; *ch 1, sk next sc, sc in next ch-1 sp; rep from *; end with ch 1, sk sc, 3 sc in next sc; rep from * around; end with ch 1, sk sc, sc in next ch-1 sp, ch 1; join with sl st in first sc; fasten off.

SQUARE II (make 15)

Rep Square I, substituting B for A and A for B.

FINISHING

Sew the squares together, alternating Square I and Square II into 5 strips with 6 squares in each strip.

Border

Rnds 1–6: With A, work 6 Seed st rnds, working 3 sc in each corner and joining at end of rnd.

Rnd 7: With B, work 1 Seed st rnd.

Rnd 8: With A, work 1 Seed st rnd.

Rnd 9: Ch 1, working from left to right (reverse sc), sc in each sc around; join with sl st to first sc; fasten off.

PILLOW

BACK AND FRONT (make 1 for each side)

With A or B, ch 50.

Foundation row (RS): Sc in 2nd ch from hook; *ch 1, sk next ch, sc in next ch; rep from * across—49 sts; turn. Work Seed st until work from beg measures approx 14", ending with Row 1; fasten off.

FINISHING

Join Front to Back

Holding WS tog, sc around 3 sides, working 3 sc in each corner; insert pillow form; sc rem side closed; join with sl st in first sc. Ch 1, working left to right (reverse sc), sc in each sc around; join with sl st in first sc; fasten off.

Design by Anna Mishka

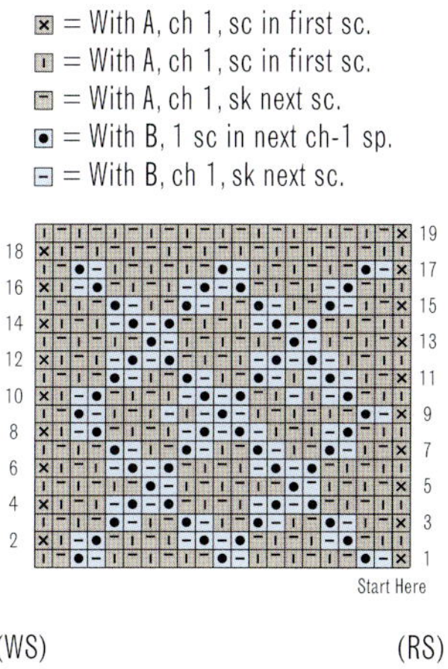

playing with blocks

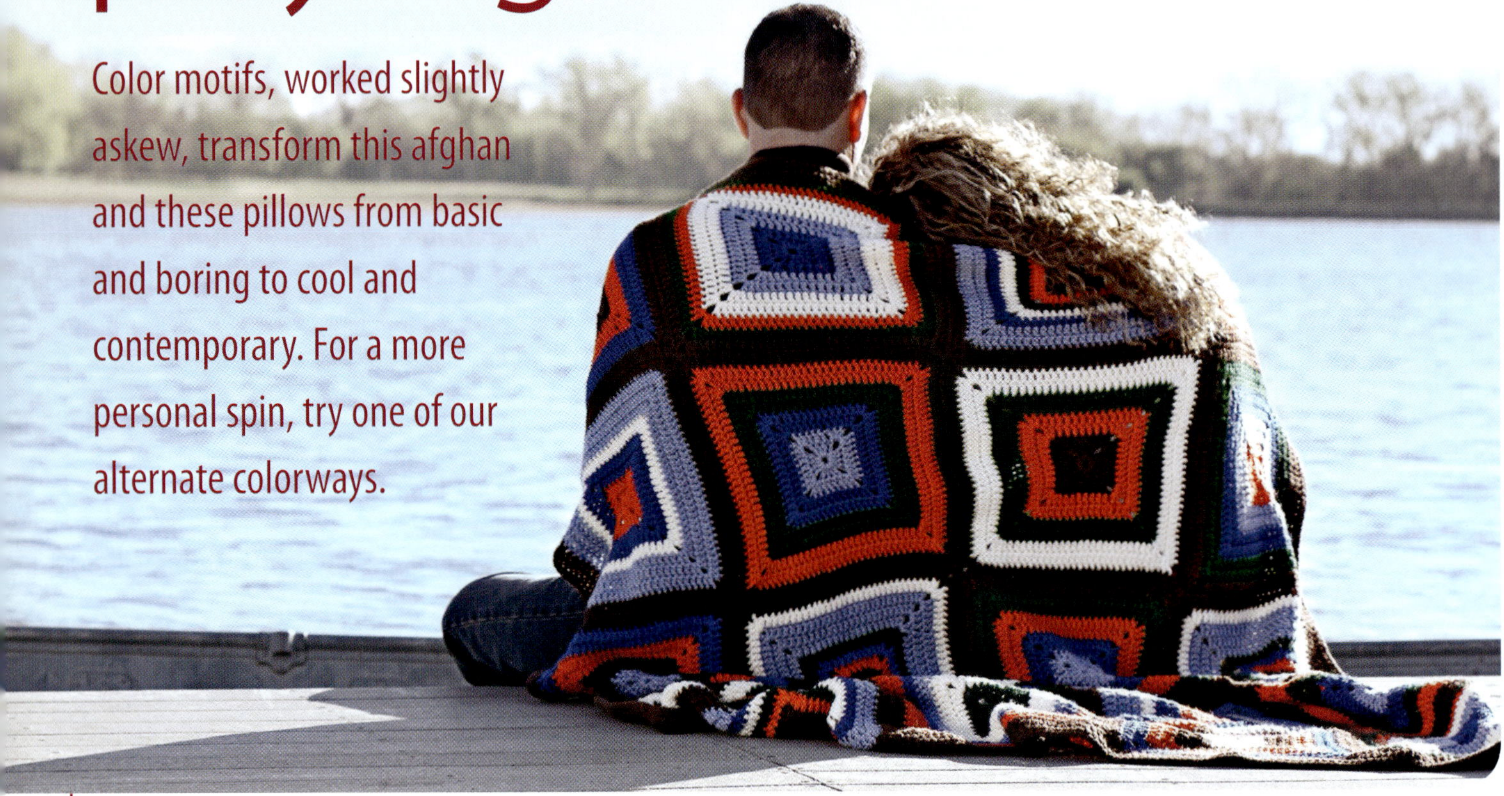

Color motifs, worked slightly askew, transform this afghan and these pillows from basic and boring to cool and contemporary. For a more personal spin, try one of our alternate colorways.

COLOR-BLOCK DECOR

SKILL LEVEL

Easy

SIZE

finished measurements

Afghan = 52×64"

Pillows = 12×12"

SHOP

yarns

Softee Chunky from Bernat (Art. 161439)

100% acrylic; 3½ oz. (100 g); 164 yds. (150 m); bulky weight

5 BULKY

For afghan

- 6 balls #39013 Dark Taupe (A)
- 3 balls #39605 Burnt Orange (B)
- 3 balls #39134 Deep Sea (C)
- 3 balls #39237 Myrtle (D)
- 3 balls #39116 Denim Heather (E)
- 2 balls #39008 Natural (F)

For pillows

- 1 ball #39013 Dark Taupe (A)
- 1 ball #39605 Burnt Orange (B)
- 1 ball #39134 Deep Sea (C)
- 1 ball #39237 Myrtle (D)
- 2 balls #39116 Denim Heather (E)
- 1 ball #39008 Natural (F)

hook & extras

- Size J/10 (6 mm) crochet hook OR SIZE NEEDED TO OBTAIN GAUGE
- Two 12"-square pillow forms
- ⅜ yard of fabric to cover each pillow form (so pillow form won't show through openwork areas)
- Blunt-end yarn needle

PREP

gauge

12 dc and 6 rows = 4" (10 cm). TAKE TIME TO CHECK YOUR GAUGE.

CROCHET

BASIC BLOCK

With first color, ch 3; join with sl st to form a ring.

Rnd 1: Ch 3—counts as dc; 3 dc in ring, (ch 2, 4 dc in ring) 3 times, ch 2; join with sl st to top of ch-3.

Rnd 2: Ch 3, dc in each of next 3 dc, (2 dc, ch 2, 2 dc) in next corner ch-2 sp, *dc in each of next 4 dc, (2 dc, ch 2, 2 dc) in next corner ch-2 sp; rep from * twice more; join with sl st to top of ch-3.

Rnd 3: Join 2nd color in any corner ch-2 sp, ch 3, (dc, ch 2, 2 dc) in same sp, *dc in each of next 8 dc, (2 dc, ch 2, 2 dc) in next corner ch-2 sp; rep from * twice more, dc in each of last 8 dc; join with sl st to top of ch-3—12 dc on each side with 4 ch-2 corner sps.

Note: To work foll rnds in same color, work sl st to next corner ch-2 sp, ch 3 for first dc and complete rnd as est.

Rnds 4–9: Cont as est, working 4 more dc on each side of each rnd—36 dc on each side with 4 ch-2 corner sps at end of Rnd 9.

AFGHAN

Note: Work 9 rnds of Basic Block in color sequences as foll.

BLOCK I (make 2)
Work 2 rnds F; 2 rnds A; 2 rnds B; 2 rnds C; 1 rnd A.

BLOCK II (make 2)
Work 2 rnds B; 2 rnds C; 1 rnd F; 3 rnds E; 1 rnd A.

BLOCK III (make 1)
Work 2 rnds E; 2 rnds D; 2 rnds B; 2 rnds C; 1 rnd A.

BLOCK IV (make 2)
Work 2 rnds A; 2 rnds B; 2 rnds D; 2 rnds F; 1 rnd A.

BLOCK V (make 2)
Work 2 rnds A; 1 rnd B; 1 rnd D; 1 rnd F; 1 rnd C; 2 rnds E; 1 rnd A.

BLOCK VI (make 2)
Work 2 rnds C; 2 rnds E; 2 rnds F; 1 rnd B; 1 rnd D; 1 rnd A.

BLOCK VII (make 2)
Work 2 rnds E; 2 rnds C; 2 rnds D; 2 rnds B; 1 rnd A.

BLOCK VIII (make 2)
Work 1 rnd A; 1 rnd B; 1 rnd C; 1 rnd D; 3 rnds E; 1 rnd F; 1 rnd A.

BLOCK IX (make 2)
Work 2 rnds B; 2 rnds E; 2 rnds C; 2 rnds D; 1 rnd A.

BLOCK X (make 2)
Work 2 rnds D; 2 rnds F; 1 rnd E; 1 rnd C; 2 rnds B; 1 rnd A.

BLOCK XI (make 1)
Work 2 rnds E; 2 rnds C; 2 rnds D; 2 rnds B; 1 rnd A.

V	X	I	VI
IV	IX	II	XI
III	VIII	VII	VIII
II	VII	IV	IX
I	VI	V	X

Placement Diagram

FINISHING

With A, sew Blocks tog in arrangement as shown in Placement Diagram, *below, left.*

Edging

Rnd 1: With RS facing, join A with sl st to any corner ch-2 sp, ch 3, (dc, ch 2, 2 dc) in same corner, *dc evenly across to next corner, (2 dc, ch 2, 2 dc) in corner; rep from * twice more, dc evenly across to end; join with sl st to top of ch-3.
Rnd 2: Sl st to first corner ch-2 sp, ch 3 and work as for Rnd 1. Fasten off. Weave in all ends.

PILLOWS (2)

BASIC BLOCK

Note: For alternative colorways for Basic Blocks, see instructions at right.

See Basic Block instructions, opposite.

FRONTS

Work one each of Block II and Block VI as for the Afghan, left.

BACKS

Work Basic Block in solid color of C for Block II pillow and E for Block VI pillow.

FINISHING

Cover pillow form with fabric.
Joining Rnd 1: With Front toward you and WS of Front and Back facing each other, join B through any corner ch-2 sp of both sides, work 3 sc in same sp; *sc in each dc across side (working through both thicknesses); 3 sc in next corner; rep from * twice more, insert pillow form, sc in each dc across rem side; join A with sl st to first sc.
Rnd 2: With A, work sc in each sc around, working 3 sc in corners; join with sl st to first sc. Fasten off. Weave in all ends.

ALTERNATIVE COLORWAYS FOR BASIC BLOCKS

Monochromatic Version (*below center, top*)
Work 2 rnds #39119 New Denim Heather; 2 rnds #39118 Denim Rag; 2 rnds #39114 Faded Denim; 2 rnds #40119 Denim Ombre; 1 rnd #39116 Denim Heather.

Stained Glass Version (*page 12, top*)
Work 2 rnds #39040 Black; 1 rnd #39330 Too Purple; 1 rnd #39132 Medium Blue; 1 rnd #39622 True
Yellow; 1 rnd #39605 Burnt Orange; 1 rnd #39728 Hot Fuchsia; 2 rnds #39040 Black.

Soft Hues Version (*below center, bottom*)
Work 2 rnds #39011 Soft Taupe; 2 rnds #39105 Pale Navy; 2 rnds #39046 Grey Heather; 2 rnds #39425 Pale Antique Rose; 1 rnd #39008 Natural.

Designs by Michelle Maks Thompson

a burst of summer

Filled with sunny blooms, this easy afghan is crocheted using just two motifs and seven colors.

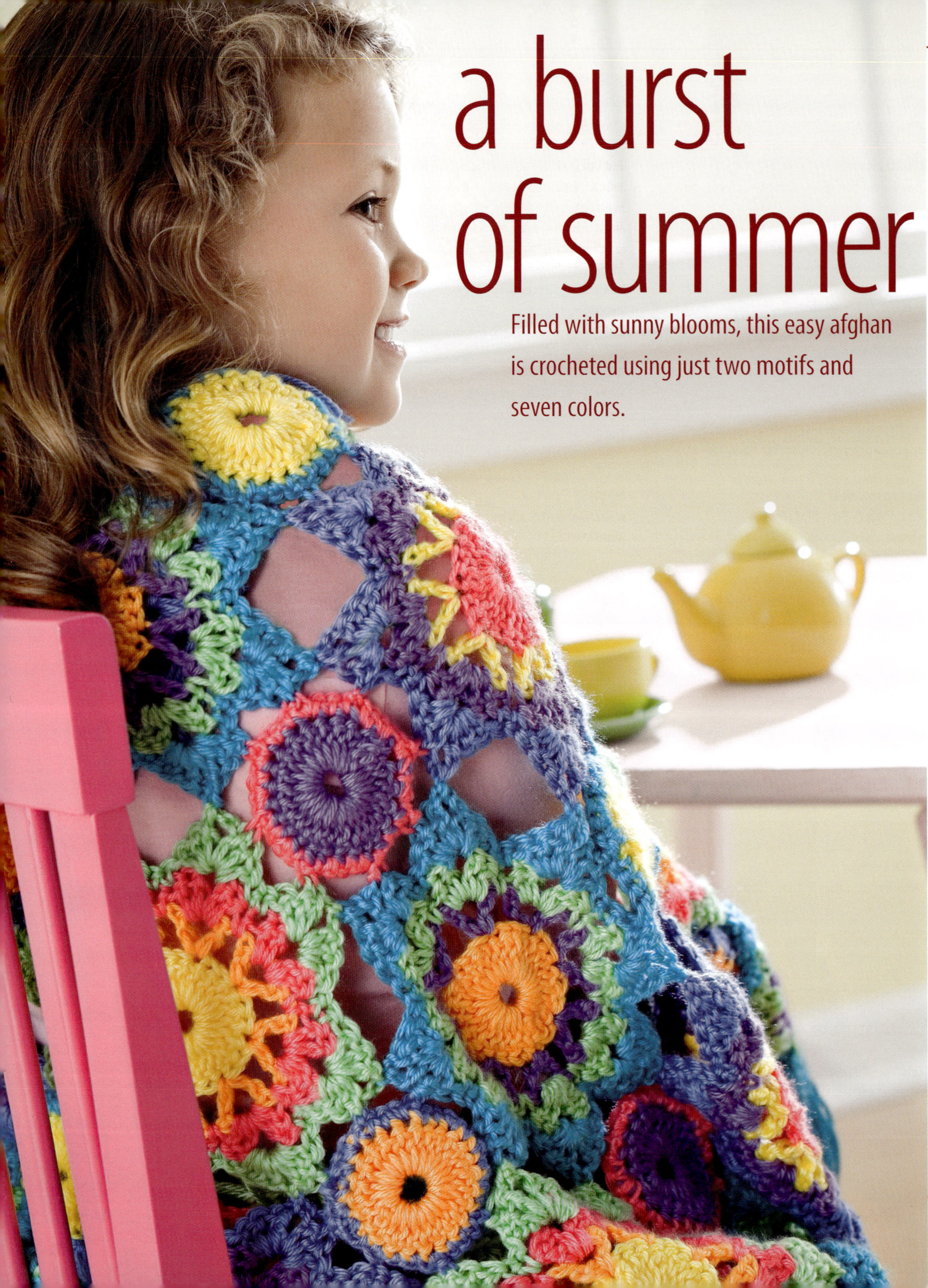

FLOWER COMFORTER

SKILL LEVEL

Easy

SIZE

finished measurements

33×44" (excluding fringe)

SHOP

yarns

Simply Soft Brites from Caron

100% acrylic; 6 oz. (172 g); 330 yds. (304 m); worsted weight

- 1 ball Watermelon #9604 (A)
- 1 ball #9605 Mango (B)
- 1 ball #9606 Lemonade (C)
- 1 ball #9607 Limelight (D)
- 1 ball #9608 Blue Mint (E)
- 1 ball #9609 Berry Blue (F)
- 1 ball #9610 Grape (G)

4 MEDIUM

Note: If adding fringe, you will need one additional ball each of D, E, and F.

hook & extra

- Size I/9 (5.5 mm) crochet hook OR SIZE NEEDED TO OBTAIN GAUGE
- Blunt-end yarn needle

PREP

gauge

Large Flower Motif = 5½" in diameter.
Small Circle Motif = 2½" in diameter.
Note: Gauge is not critical for this project.

CROCHET

Note: To join a new color, complete the stitch in progress until 2 loops remain on the hook, drop the color in use; with new color, yarn over, and draw it through the 2 loops on the hook.

LARGE FLOWER (make 48)

Work Rnds 1–4 in the foll colorways:
Colorway 1 (make 16): Beg ch and Rnd 1 (C), Rnd 2 (B), Rnd 3 (A), Rnd 4 (D).
Colorway 2 (make 16): Beg ch and Rnd 1 (B), Rnd 2 (G), Rnd 3 (D), Rnd 4 (E).
Colorway 3 (make 16): Beg ch and Rnd 1 (A), Rnd 2 (C), Rnd 3 (G), Rnd 4 (F).
With first color, ch 6, join with a sl st to form ring.
Rnd 1 (RS): Ch 2—counts as dc; 23 dc in ring, join 2nd color, and join it with sl st to top of beg ch-2—24 dc. Fasten off first color.
Rnd 2: With 2nd color, ch 4—counts as dc, ch 2; dc in same st, ch 1, *sk next 2 dc, (dc, ch 2, dc) in next dc, ch 1; rep from * 6 more times, sk next 2 dc, join 3rd color with sl st to 2nd ch of beg ch-4; fasten off 2nd color.
Rnd 3: With 3rd color, ch 2—counts as dc; dc in next ch-2 sp, ch 2, 2 dc in same sp, *sc in ch-1 sp, (2 dc, ch 2, 2 dc) in next ch-2 sp; rep from * 6 more times, end sc in ch-1 sp, join 4th color with sl st to top of beg ch-2; fasten off 3rd color.
Rnd 4: With 4th color, sl st in first ch-2 sp, ch 2—counts as dc; (2 dc, ch 1, 3 dc) in same sp, *sc in sp on each side of next sc; (3 dc, ch 1, 3 dc) in next ch-2 sp; rep from * 6 more times, sc in sp on each side of next sc, and join with sl st to top of beg ch-2; fasten off. Weave in ends.

SMALL CIRCLE (make 35)

Work Rnds 1–2 in the foll colorways:
Colorway 1 (make 11): Beg ch and Rnd 1 (C), Rnd 2 (E).
Colorway 2 (make 12): Beg ch and Rnd 1 (B), Rnd 2 (F).
Colorway 3 (make 12): Beg ch and Rnd 1 (G), Rnd 2 (A). With first color, ch 6, join with sl st to form ring.
Rnd 1 (RS): Ch 2—counts as dc; 23 dc in ring, join 2nd color with sl st to top of beg ch-2—24 dc; fasten off first color.
Rnd 2: Using 2nd color, *sc in next 2 sts, 2 sc in next st; rep from * around; join with sl st to first sc; fasten off. Weave in ends.

FINISHING

Assemble Large Flower Rows

Foll Assembly Diagram, *right*, lay out one row of 6 Large Flowers; pin each Flower to the one beside it at the two points where they touch (see photo, *opposite*). Using yarn needle and yarn color to match one of the Flowers, sew the points together. Cont laying out and sewing each row of Large Flowers, foll the Assembly Diagram—8 rows of 6 Flowers each. Join first and 2nd rows and cont joining rows until all 8 rows are sewn together.

Attach Small Circles

Lay completed piece on a flat surface; foll Assembly Diagram, position the first row of Small Circles between Large Flowers; pin in place. Using yarn needle and matching yarn color, attach Small Circles bet the points of the Large Flower Circles. Cont until each row of Small Circles has been attached.

Fringe

Cut 13" strands of D, E, and F.
Working around entire Afghan, make 7 Fringes evenly around each unattached petal and 3 Fringes along the side of each attached petal as folls: Matching colors of Rnd 4, hold 2 strands tog and fold in half. *Insert hook from WS to RS into st or ch-1 sp, pull lps through, insert ends into lp and pull tight against edge; rep from *. Trim if necessary.

Design by Marilyn Losee

Assembly Diagram

go team!

Be a sport and craft this bedspread and pillow set for that special little guy. The base squares are worked in single crochet—the dark ones with vertical stripes of cross-stitching to simulate plaid. All team logos are cut from pennants and sewn or glued on.

SPORTY SET

SKILL LEVEL

Easy

SIZE

finished measurements

Bedspread = 50×60" (excluding borders)
Pillow = 14" square (excluding borders)

SHOP

yarns

Softee Chunky Solids from Bernat (Art. 161439)
100% acrylic; 3½ oz. (100 g); 164 yds. (150 m); chunky weight

5 BULKY

For bedspread

- 6 balls #39114 Faded Denim (A)
- 3 balls #39705 Berry Red (B)
- 2 balls #39011 Soft Taupe (C)

For pillow

- 1 ball #39114 Faded Denim (A)
- 1 ball #39705 Berry Red (B)
- 1 ball #39011 Soft Taupe (C)
- 1 ball #39008 Natural (D)

hook & extras

- Size J/10 (6 mm) crochet hook OR SIZE NEEDED TO OBTAIN GAUGE
- 14" pillow form
- Assorted appliqués (sample uses WinCraft Sports officially licensed pennants, cutting decorative sections from a variety of pennants)
- Sewing needle and thread OR fabric glue (such as Fabri-Tek)
- Blunt-end yarn needle

PREP

gauge

27 sc and 34 rows = 10". TAKE TIME TO CHECK YOUR GAUGE.

CROCHET BEDSPREAD

Note: Bedspread is worked in 5 strips; strips are then sewn or slip-stitched tog.

STRIP I (make 3)

Color Sequence I: Work *(4 rows A, 2 rows B, 4 rows A, 2 rows C) twice, 4 rows A, 2 rows B, 4 rows A, 34 rows D; rep from * twice more.
With A, ch 29, sc in 2nd ch from hook and in each ch across—28 sts; turn.
Row 1: Ch 1, sc in each sc across. Cont to rep Row 1 until Color Sequence I is complete—204 rows; fasten off.

STRIP II (make 2)

Color Sequence II: Work *34 rows D, (4 rows A, 2 rows B, 4 rows A, 2 rows C) twice, 4 rows A, 2 rows B, 4 rows A; rep from * twice more.
With D, ch 29. Work same as Strip I, foll Color Sequence II.

FINISHING

Work 6 rows of cross-stitches to complete the plaid pattern on striped blocks as foll: Beg stitching in 2nd row and in 2nd st from left side of block with C. Work towards top of block and make a cross-stitch in every other row—17 cross-stitches.
Sk 4 sts to right of first row of C cross-stitches and work B cross-stitch in next st.
Complete row of B cross-stitches—17 cross-stitches.
Cont to make 4 more rows of cross-stitches to complete plaid pat, alternating colors B and C. Work cross-stitches in the same manner in all colored blocks. Alternate strips, beg and ending with Strip I; join strips.

Side Edges

With RS facing and working at side edge, (join A and sc evenly along side of plaid section, join D and sc evenly along side of solid section) 3 times; fasten off. Rep on opposite side edge.

Border

Join B in any sc.
Rnd 1 (RS): Ch 1, sc evenly around entire Bedspread, working 3 sc in each corner; end join with sl st to first sc; turn.
Rnds 2–3 (WS): Ch 1, sc in each sc around, working 3 sc in each corner; join it with sl st to top of first sc; do not turn; fasten off at end of Rnd 3. Weave in loose ends.
Cut appliqués into desired shapes. Sew or glue shapes onto solid D sections of Bedspread.

PILLOW

FRONT

With D, ch 38. Sc in 2nd ch from hook and in each ch across—37 sts.
Row 1: Ch 1, sc in each sc across.
Rep Row 1 for a total of 46 rows; fasten off.

Side Edges and Border

With RS facing and D, sc evenly along each side edge of Pillow.
Join B in any sc and work 3 rnds sc same as for Bedspread.

BACK

Color Sequence: Work (4 rows A, 2 rows B, 4 rows A, 2 rows C) 3 times; 4 rows A, 2 rows B, 4 rows A.
With A, ch 38. Sc in 2nd ch from hook and in each ch across—37 sts.
Cont rep Row 1 until color sequence is complete—46 rows; fasten off.

Side Edges and Border

With RS facing and A, sc evenly along each side edge of Pillow. Join B in any sc and work 3 rnds sc same as for Bedspread.

FINISHING

Work 8 rows of cross-stitch embroidery in the same manner as for Bedspread. Sew desired appliqué(s) on front of Pillow.
Sew 3 sides of Pillow tog, insert pillow form, sew rem side closed.

Design by Michelle Maks Thompson

baby joys

Your heart simply overflows with love for that little newborn. Show her or him your affection with one of these adorable handmades.

on a roll

Soft and safe, this 8-inch ball is made from six wedges that are crocheted together and then capped, top and bottom, with crochet circles.

BABY-SAFE BALL

SKILL LEVEL

Easy

SIZE

finished measurement

Circumference (stuffed) = 23"

SHOP

yarns

Babysoft from Lion Brand (Art. 920)
60% acrylic, 40% nylon; 5 oz. (140 g); 459 yds. (413 m); DK weight

- 1 ball #176 Spring Green (A)
- 1 ball #157 Pastel Yellow (B)
- 1 ball #143 Lavender (C)
- 1 ball #100 White (D)

3 LIGHT

hook & extras

- Size I/9 (5.5 mm) crochet hook OR SIZE NEEDED TO OBTAIN GAUGE
- Polyester fiberfill
- Blunt-end yarn needle

PREP

gauge

With a double strand of yarn, 12 sc and 16 rows = 4" (10 cm). TAKE TIME TO CHECK YOUR GAUGE.

Note: Use a double strand of yarn throughout the entire project.

CROCHET

PANEL (make 6; 2 each with A, B, and C)

With A, ch 4.

Row 1: Sc in 2nd ch from hook and in each ch across—3 sts; turn.

Row 2: Ch 1, sc in each sc across; turn.

Row 3: Ch 1, sc in each sc across, ending 2 sc in last sc—4 sts; turn.

Rows 4–6: Rep Row 3—7 sts.

Row 7: Rep Row 2.

Rows 8–9: Rep Row 3—9 sts.

Rows 10–11: Rep Row 2.

Rows 12–13: Rep Row 3—11 sts.

Rows 14–19: Rep Row 2.

Row 20: Ch 1, sk sc, sc across—10 sts; turn.

Row 21: Rep Row 20—9 sts.

Rows 22–23: Rep Row 2.

Rows 24–25: Rep Row 20—7 sts.

Row 26: Rep Row 2.

Rows 27–30: Rep Row 20—3 sts.

Row 31: Rep Row 2. Fasten off.

END (make 2)

With D, ch 2.

Rnd 1: Work 6 sc in 2nd ch from hook.

Rnd 2: Work 2 sc in each sc around—12 sts.

Rnd 3: (Sc in sc, 2 sc in next sc) around—18 sts.

Rnd 4: (Sc in 2 sc, 2 sc in next sc) around—24 sts. Fasten off.

FINISHING

Alternating color Panels, hold 2 Panels tog and with D, sc across to join; turn.

Sl st in each sc across. Fasten off. Rep until all Panels are joined. Stuff ball with fiberfill.

Sew Ends to ball, covering edges of Panels.

Design by Linda Cyr

so precious

Present this pretty blanket to a mom-to-be, and her oohs and aahs—and heartfelt thanks—are guaranteed. Shown here in pastel colors, it would be lovely all in white, too.

BERIBBONED BLANKET

SKILL LEVEL

Easy

SIZE

finished measurements

30×40"

SHOP

yarns

Softee Baby Ombre from Bernat (Art. 166031)
100% acrylic; 4½ oz. (120 g);
380 yds. (345 m); DK weight
• 2 balls #02150 Chiffon Print (MC)

Softee Baby Solid from Bernat (Art. 166030)
100% acrylic; 5 oz. (140 g);
455 yds. (416 m); DK weight
• 1 ball #02004 Mint (A)

hook & extras

- Size H/8 (5 mm) crochet hook OR SIZE NEEDED TO OBTAIN GAUGE
- 4½ yards of ¼"-wide satin ribbon
- Blunt-end yarn needle

PREP

gauge

4 lps and 9 rows = 4" (10 cm) in scallop pat.
TAKE TIME TO CHECK YOUR GAUGE.

CROCHET

With MC, ch 122.

Foundation row: Sc in 2nd ch from hook, *ch 5, sk 4 ch, sc in next ch; rep from * across—24 lps. Turn.

Row 1 (RS): Ch 3, 2 dc in first sc—counts as 3 dc; sc in next ch-5 lp, *ch 5, sc in next ch-5 lp; in next sc work 2 dc, ch 1, 2 dc—scallop made; sc in next ch-5 lp; rep from * across; end ch 5, sc in last ch-5 lp, 3 dc in last sc; turn.

Row 2: Ch 1, sc in first dc, ch 5, sc in next ch-5 lp; *ch 5, sc in ch-1 sp of next scallop, ch 5, sc in next ch-5 lp; rep from * across, end ch 5, sc in 3rd ch of turning ch; turn.

Row 3: Ch 5—counts as dc and ch 2; *sc in next ch-5 lp, work scallop in next sc, sc in next ch-5 lp, ch 5; rep from * across; end last rep with ch 2 instead of ch 5, dc in last sc; turn.

Row 4: Ch 1, sc in first dc, ch 5, *sc in ch-1 sp of next scallop, ch 5, sc in next ch-5 lp; rep from * across, end with last sc in 3rd ch of turning ch-5; turn.

Rep Rows 1–4 for scallop pat until piece measures 40", ending with Row 3 of pat.

Last row: Ch 1, sc in first dc, ch 4, *sc in ch-1 sp of next scallop, ch 4, sc in next ch-5 lp; rep from * across, ending with last sc in 3rd ch of turning ch-5; turn. Do not fasten off. Cont as foll for border:

Border

Rnd 1 (RS): Ch 1, work 2 sc in first sc, *4 sc in next ch-4 lp, sc in next sc; rep from * across, work 3 sc in last sc for corner; working along next side work 2 sc around side of next dc, **sc in side of next row, 2 sc around side of next turning ch or dc**; rep from ** to ** across, 3 sc in next corner, rep from * across foundation-ch edge and then from ** to ** along opposite side edge; sc in same sc as first 2 sc of rnd, join with sl st to first sc; fasten off.

Rnd 2: Join A with sl st in center sc of any corner, ch 1, 2 sc in same sp; sc in each sc around, working 3 sc in center sc of each corner, sc in same sc as first 2 sc of rnd, join with sl st to first sc.

Rnd 3: Sl st in center sc of corner, ch 3, 2 dc in same sp, ch 1, sk next sc, *dc in each of next 2 sc, ch 1, sk next sc; rep from * to next corner, work 3 dc in corner. Cont in same manner around entire blanket, join with sl st to 3rd ch of starting ch-3.

Rnd 4: Sl st in center dc of corner, ch 3, work 2 dc in same sc, ch 2, sc in next ch-1 sp, *ch 4, sc in next ch-1 sp; rep from * to next corner, ch 2, work 3 dc in center dc of next corner, ch 2, sc in next ch-1 sp.

Cont in same manner around entire blanket, join with sl st to 3rd ch of starting ch-3.

Rnd 5: Sl st to center dc of corner, ch 4, work (dc, ch 1) 3 times, and dc in same st, sc in next ch-2 sp; *in next ch-4 sp work (dc, ch 1) 4 times and dc—edge scallop made; sc in next ch-4 sp; rep from * to next corner, working sc in last ch-2 sp before corner; work edge scallop in center dc of corner.

Cont in same manner around entire blanket, join with sl st to 3rd ch of starting ch-4; fasten off.

Design by Bobbi Anderson

little lambkin

With no buttons or loose parts that might come off, this fleecy little fellow is as perfect for babies as it is for older tots.

LAMB TOY

SKILL LEVEL

Easy

SIZE

finished measurements

15" long and 10" high

SHOP

yarn

Jiffy from Lion Brand (Art. 450)
100% acrylic; 3 oz. (85 g); 135 yds. (123 m); bulky weight

- 2 balls #099 Fisherman

6 SUPER BULKY

hook & extras

- Size J/10 (6 mm) crochet hook OR SIZE NEEDED TO OBTAIN GAUGE
- Brown tapestry yarn
- Polyester stuffing
- Blunt-end yarn needle

PREP

gauge

11 sc and 13 rows = 4" (10 cm). TAKE TIME TO CHECK YOUR GAUGE.

stitch abbreviations

Sc2tog = Draw up a loop in each of next 2 stitches, yarn over and draw through both loops on hook.
Sc3tog = Draw up a loop in each of next 3 stitches, yarn over and draw through all loops on hook—2-stitch decrease made.

CROCHET

PATTERN STITCH

Bobble Pattern (multiple of 2 sts + 1)

Row 1 (WS): Ch 1, sc in first sc; *tr in next sc, sc in next sc; rep from * across, noting that sc is worked tightly after tr and then pushed to RS to form the bobble; turn.

Row 2: Ch 1, sc in each st across; turn.

Row 3: Ch 1, sc in first 2 sc; *tr in next sc, sc in next sc; rep from * across, ending tr in next sc, sc in last 2 sc; turn.

Row 4: Rep Row 2.

Rep Rows 1–4 for Bobble pat.

LAMB BODY

Head

Beg at tip of nose, ch 2.

Rnd 1 (RS): Work 6 sc in 2nd ch from hook; join with sl st to first sc.

Rnd 2: Ch 1, 2 sc in each sc around—12 sc; join.

Rnd 3: Ch 1, sc in first 5 sc, 2 sc in each of next 3 sc, sc in last 4 sc—15 sc; join.

Rnd 4: Ch 1, sc in first 6 sc, 2 sc in each of next 3 sc, sc in last 6 sc—18 sc; join.

Rnds 5–7: Ch 1, sc in each sc around; join.

Rnd 8: Ch 1, sc in first 6 sc, 2 sc in each of next 6 sc, sc in last 6 sc—24 sc; join.

Rnd 9: Ch 1, sc in each sc around; join.

Rnd 10: Ch 1, sc in first 11 sc, 2 sc in next sc, sc in last 12 sc—25 sc; join.

Body

Turn work, cont in rows as foll:

Row 1 (WS): Work Row 1 of Bobble pat.

Row 2: Ch 1, (sc in next 8 sc, 2 sc in next sc) twice, sc in last 7 sc—27 sc; turn.

Row 3: Work Row 3 of Bobble pat.

Row 4: Ch 1, (sc in next 8 sc, 2 sc in next sc) twice, sc in last 9 sc—29 sc; turn.

Row 5: Work Row 1 of Bobble pat.

Row 6: Ch 1, (sc in 5 sc, 2 sc in next sc) 4 times, sc in last 5 sc—33 sc; turn.

Cont in Bobble pat and inc one st each end of next 2 RS rows and include new sts into pat—37 sts. Work even until piece from tip of nose measures approx 11", ending with Row 1 or Row 3 of Bobble pat.

Shape Back

Cont Bobble pat.

Row 1 (RS): Ch 1, sc in first 15 sts, sc2tog, sc3tog, sc2tog, sc in last 15 sts—33 sts; turn.

Row 2: Work even.

Row 3: Ch 1, sc in first 13 sts, sc2tog, sc3tog, sc2tog, sc in last 13 sts—29 sts; turn.

Row 4: Work even.

Row 5: Ch 1, sc in first 11 sts, sc2tog, sc3tog, sc2tog, sc in last 11 sts—25 sts; turn.

Row 6: Work even.

Row 7: Ch 1, sc in first 9 sts, sc2tog, sc3tog, sc2tog, sc in last 9 sts—21 sts; fasten off. Fold last row in half and sew tog. Place markers 1½" on either side of seam at open edges.

BODY BASE

Ch 10.

Row 1 (RS): Sc in 2nd ch from hook and in each ch across—9 sc; turn.

Row 2: Ch 1, 2 sc in first sc, sc in each sc across, ending 2 sc in last sc—11 sc; turn.

Cont in sc on 11 sts until piece measures approx 4½" from beg, ending with a WS row.

Shape Side

Row 1: Ch 1, sc2tog, sc in each sc across, ending sc2tog; turn.

Rows 2–4: Ch 1, sc in each sc across; turn. Rep last 4 rows 3 more times—3 sc; turn.

Next row: Ch 1, sc in 3 sc; turn.

Last row: Ch 1, sc3tog; fasten off.

LEGS (make 4)

Ch 2.

Rnd 1 (RS): 6 sc in 2nd ch from hook; join with sl st to first sc.

Rnd 2: Ch 1, 2 sc in each sc around—12 sc; join.

Rnd 3: Ch 1, sc in back lp of each sc around; join.

Rnds 4–5: Ch 1; sc in each sc around; join.

Rnd 6: Ch 1, (sc in 2 sc, sc2tog) 3 times—9 sc; join.

Rnds 7–9: Ch 1, sc in each sc around; join.

After Rnd 9, fasten off. Stuff Legs.

TAIL

Ch 2.

Rnd 1 (RS): Work 4 sc in 2nd ch from hook; join with sl st to first sc.

Rnds 2–5: Ch 1, sc in each sc around; join. Fasten off at end of Rnd 5. Stuff Tail.

EARS (make 2)

Ch 5. With RS facing, sc in 2nd ch from hook, sc in next 2 ch, 4 hdc in last ch; working along opposite side of foundation ch, sc in next 3 ch; fasten off.

FINISHING

Leaving an opening for stuffing, sew Base to Body, matching point of Base at neck and matching corners of foundation row to markers on Body. Stuff; sew opening closed. Sew back Legs to Base one row from side and back sc edges. Sew front Legs to Base close to 4th bobble row. Position Ears behind first bobble row and bet 3rd and 4th bobbles and centered behind 7th bobble; sew in place. Center Tail onto hind end behind 13th bobble row and sew in place.

Embroider Features

Refer to photo and use tapestry yarn for embroidery.

Nose: Make 5 straight stitches from center of Rnd 1 down to beg of Rnd 2.

Mouth: Make one long straight st on each side of nose, over Rnd 2 with 3 sc bet.

Eyes: Make 5 straight sts slightly angled to outside, using nose as center mark and 3 sc bet on Rnd 6.

Brows: Make 5 stem sts in rnd above each eye; add 3 straight sts at outer edges for lashes.

Design by Gayle Bunn

splashy duo

Babies go through washcloths and towels almost as fast as they do diapers. So for bath-time fun, only these soft accessories will do.

WASHCLOTH & TOWEL

SKILL LEVEL

Easy

SIZE

finished measurements

Washcloth = 9×9"

Hooded Towel = 32×32"

SHOP

yarns

Crystal Palace Cotton Chenille

100% cotton; 1¾ oz. (50 g); 98 yds. (89 m); worsted weight

- 7 balls #5509 Pink (A)
- 1 ball #3646 Yellow (B)
- 2 balls #5960 Lilac (C)

4 MEDIUM

hook & extra

- Size G/6 (4 mm) crochet hook OR SIZE NEEDED TO OBTAIN GAUGE
- Blunt-end yarn needle

PREP

gauge

12 sc and 12 rows = 4" (10 cm). TAKE TIME TO CHECK YOUR GAUGE.

special stitch

Picot = In next single crochet, work single crochet, chain 2, and slip stitch.

Note: This yarn relaxes after it has been crocheted, so the projects may end up slightly larger than the finished measurements indicated above.

CROCHET

WASHCLOTH

With A, ch 22.

Row 1: Sc in 2nd ch from hook and in each ch across—21 sts; turn.

Row 2: Ch 1, sc in each sc across; turn.

Rep Row 2 for 19 more times—21 total rows.

Fasten off.

Border

Rnd 1: With RS facing, join B with sl st in top right sc, ch 1, 3 sc in same sc; (19 sc along edge, 3 sc in corner) 3 times, 19 sc along edge; join with sl st in first sc. Fasten off.

Rnd 2: With RS facing, join C with sl st in center sc of right corner, ch 1, 3 sc in same sc; (21 sc along edge, 3 sc in corner) 3 times, 21 sc along edge.

Rnd 3: Sc in next sc, 3 sc in next sc; (23 sc along edge, 3 sc in corner) 3 times, 22 sc along last edge; join. Fasten off.

Rnd 4: With RS facing, join A with sl st in center sc of right corner, ch 1, in same sc work sc, ch 2, and sl st—picot made. *Sc in next 5 sc, (picot in next sc, sc in next 6 sc) twice, picot in next sc, sc in next 5 sc**, picot in corner sc; rep from * around, ending last rep at **; join with sl st in first sc. Fasten off.

HOODED TOWEL

HOOD

With A, ch 4.

Row 1: Sc in 2nd ch from hook, 3 sc in next ch, sc in last ch—5 sc; turn.

Row 2: Ch 1, 2 sc in first sc, sc in each sc across, ending 2 sc in last sc—7 sc; turn.

Row 3: Ch 1, sc in first 3 sc, 3 sc in next sc, sc in last 3 sc—9 sc; turn.

Row 4: Rep Row 2—11 sc; turn.

Row 5: Ch 1, sc in first 5 sc, 3 sc in next sc, sc in last 5 sc—13 sc; turn.

Row 6: Ch 1, sc in first 6 sc, 3 sc in next sc, sc in last 6 sc—15 sc. Cont in pat as est until there are 39 sts.

Do not turn. Ch 1, work 18 sc evenly spaced along side to point, 3 sc in point, 18 sc evenly spaced along opposite edge. Fasten off.

With RS facing, join B with sl st at lower edge, ch 1, work 41 sc evenly spaced across. Fasten off. With C, work 2 sc rows.

Picot Edge

With RS facing, join A with sl st in first sc, ch 1, sc in same sc and next sc; *picot in next sc, sc in next 5 sc; rep from * across, ending picot in next sc, sc in last 2 sc. Fasten off.

TOWEL BODY

With A, ch 86.

Row 1: Sc in 2nd ch from hook and in each ch across—85 sts; turn.

Row 2: Ch 1, sc in each sc across; turn.

Rep Row 2 for 83 more times—total of 85 rows from Row 1.

Border

Rnd 1: With A, ch 1, 3 sc in first sc, sc in next 83 sc, 3 sc in last sc. Work 83 sc along each edge with 3 sc in each corner, ending before first corner. Join with sl st in first sc.

Rnd 2: Ch 1, sc in same sc as joining, 3 sc in next sc; (work 85 sc along edge, 3 sc in corner) 3 times, 84 sc along last edge; join.

Rnd 3: Ch 1, sc in first 2 sc, 3 sc in next sc; (work 87 sc along edge, 3 sc in corner) 3 times, 85 sc along last edge; join.

Rnd 4: Ch 1, sc in first 3 sc, 3 sc in next sc; (work 89 sc along edge, 3 sc in corner) 3 times, 86 sc along last edge; join.

Rnd 5: Ch 1, sc in first 4 sc, 3 sc in next sc; (work 91 sc along edge; 3 sc in corner) 3 times, 87 sc along last edge; join. Fasten off.

Rnd 6: With RS facing, join B with sl st in center sc of corner, ch 1, 3 sc in same sc. (Work 93 sc along edge, 3 sc in corner) 3 times, 93 sc along last edge; join. Fasten off.

Rnd 7: With RS facing, join C with sl st in center sc of corner, ch 1, 3 sc in same sc. (Work 95 sc along edge, 3 sc in corner) 3 times, 95 sc along last edge; join.

Rnd 8: Ch 1, sc in first sc; (3 sc in next sc, sc in next 97 sc) 3 times, 3 sc in next sc, sc in 96 sc; join.

Rnd 9 (joining Hood to Body): Ch 1, sc in 2 sc, 3 sc in next sc, sc in next 76 sc.

Holding WS of Hood to RS of Body and working through both layers, sc in next 23 sts, 3 sc in next st, sc through next 23 sts, then sc in next 76 sts along side. Work 3 sc in next sc, sc in next 99 sts, 3 sc in next sc, sc in rem 97 sts; join. Fasten off.

Rnd 10: With RS facing, join A with sl st in center sc of corner, ch 1, in same sc make sc, ch 2, sl st in same sc—beg picot made.

(Sc in next 5 sc, picot in next sc) around, ending last rep with sc in 5 sc; join. Fasten off.

Designs by Ann E. Smith

blanketed in love

Boy or girl? Doesn't matter! This design blends together two colors—one in a velvety suede yarn; the other in a traditional baby yarn—for a blanket that's subtly shaded and extra thick.

CUDDLY BLANKET

SKILL LEVEL
Easy

SIZE

finished measurements

41½×42"

SHOP

yarns

Babysoft from Lion Brand (Art. 920)
60% acrylic, 40% nylon; 5 oz. (140 g); 459 yds. (413 m); DK weight
- 2 balls #106 Pastel Blue (A)
- 2 balls #143 Lavender (B)

Velvetspun from Lion Brand (Art. 580)
100% polyester; 3 oz. (85 g); 54 yds. (49 m); chunky weight
- 2 balls #106 Bluebell (C)

hook & extra
- Size K/10½ (6.5 mm) crochet hook OR SIZE NEEDED TO OBTAIN GAUGE
- Blunt-end yarn needle

PREP

gauge

With 1 strand each of A and B held tog, 10 dc and 6 rows = 4" (10 cm). TAKE TIME TO CHECK YOUR GAUGE.

CROCHET

BODY

With 1 strand each of A and B held tog, ch 101.

Row 1 (RS): Dc in 4th ch from hook and in each ch across—99 sts; turn.

Row 2: Ch 3—counts as dc; dc in each dc across; turn.

Rep Row 2 until Blanket measures 40" from beg. Fasten off A and B.

Edging

Rnd 1: With RS facing, join C with a sl st in top right corner st, ch 1; *in corner st work sc, ch 1, and sc; (ch 1, sk dc, sc in next st) across, end with ch 1, sk dc, in last dc work sc, ch 1, and sc for corner.

Ch 1, working across side edge, work sc in each row across and make ch 1 bet each sc; ch 1 before working next corner; rep from * around; join with a sl st in first sc.

Rnd 2: Ch 1, sc in first sc, 2 sc in corner ch-1 sp. Sc in each sc and ch-1 sp around, working 2 sc in each corner ch-1 sp; join with a sl st in first sc. Fasten off.

Design by Michelle Maks Thompson

fashion accents

Get ready for a season of fresh style—for the whole family—with accessories that boast great shapes, bold textures, and super colors.

one scarf 5 ways

A single pattern is all you need to create an entire scarf wardrobe. The secret lies in working with various yarn combinations and textures.

1. TURQUOISE SCARF

SKILL LEVEL

Beginner

SIZE

finished measurements

4×60"

SHOP

yarn

Cha Cha from Patons (Art. 242002)
100% nylon; 1¾ oz. (50 g); 77 yds. (70 m); bulky weight
- 2 balls #02742 R and B

6 SUPER BULKY

hook & extra

- Size K/10 (6 mm) crochet hook OR SIZE NEEDED TO OBTAIN GAUGE
- Blunt-end yarn needle

PREP

gauge

15 sts and 6 rows = 4" (10 cm) in (ch-1, dc) pat.

TAKE TIME TO CHECK YOUR GAUGE.

Note: To work dc around turning ch of previous row, yo, insert hook from front to back to front around turning ch, yo and draw up a lp, (yo and draw through 2 lps on hook) twice.

CROCHET

Ch 18.

Row 1: Dc in 6th ch from hook, (ch 1, sk next ch, dc in next ch) 6 times—7 ch-1 sps. Ch 2—counts as first dc of next row; turn.

Row 2: Dc in first ch-1 sp, (ch 1, dc in next ch-1 sp) 6 times, dc around turning ch of previous row (see Note above)—6 ch-1 sps. Ch 3—counts as first dc and ch-1 of next row; turn.

Row 3: Dc in first ch-1 sp, (ch 1, dc in next ch-1 sp) 5 times, ch 1, dc around turning ch of previous row—7 ch-1 sps. Ch 2; turn.

Rep Rows 2–3 until piece measures 60" or desired length from beg; fasten off. Use yarn needle to weave in the ends.

2. PINK SCARF

SKILL LEVEL

Beginner

SIZE

finished measurements

4½×60"

SHOP

yarns

Lacette from Patons (Art. 243030)
39% nylon, 36% acrylic, 25% mohair;
1¾ oz. (50 g); 235 yds. (215 m); fine weight
2 FINE
- 1 ball #30440 Precious Pink (A)

Glittalic from Patons (Art. 241066)
95% polyester, 5% lurex; 1¾ oz. (50 g);
61 yds. (55 m); chunky weight
5 BULKY
- 2 balls #66405 Maroon Shine (B)

hook & extra

- Size L/11 (8 mm) crochet hook OR SIZE NEEDED TO OBTAIN GAUGE
- Blunt-end yarn needle

PREP

gauge

13 sts and 6 rows = 4" (10 cm) over (ch-1, dc) st with A and B held tog as one. TAKE TIME TO CHECK YOUR GAUGE.

Note: To work dc around turning ch of previous row, yo, insert hook from front to back to front around turning ch, yo and draw up a lp, (yo and draw through 2 lps on hook) twice.

CROCHET

With A and B held tog as one, ch 18.

Row 1: Dc in 6th ch from hook, (ch 1, sk next ch, dc in next ch) 6 times—7 ch-1 sps. Ch 2—counts as first dc of next row; turn.

Row 2: Dc in first ch-1 sp, (ch 1, dc in next ch-1 sp) 6 times, dc around turning ch of previous row (see Note below left)—6 ch-1 sps. Ch 3—counts as first dc and ch-1 of next row; turn.

Row 3: Dc in first ch-1 sp, (ch 1, dc in next ch-1 sp) 5 times, ch 1, dc around turning ch of previous row—7 ch-1 sps. Ch 2; turn.

Rep Rows 2–3 until piece measures 60" or desired length from beg; fasten off. Use yarn needle to weave in the ends.

3. CREAM SCARF

SKILL LEVEL

Beginner

SIZE

finished measurements

5×60"

SHOP

yarns

Brilliant from Patons (Art. 246103)
69% acrylic, 19% nylon, 12% polyester;
1¾ oz. (50 g); 166 yds. (151 m); DK weight
3 LIGHT
- 2 balls #03008 Crystal Cream (A)

Glittalic from Patons (Art. 241066)
95% polyester, 5% lurex; 1¾ oz. (50 g);
61 yds. (55 m); chunky weight
5 BULKY
- 2 balls #66008 Cream Gleam (B)

Lacette from Patons (Art. 243030)
39% nylon, 36% acrylic, 25% mohair;
1¾ oz. (50 g); 235 yds. (215 m);
fine weight
2 FINE
- 1 ball #30008 Cream Caress (C)

hook & extra

- Size N/15 (10 mm) crochet hook OR SIZE NEEDED TO OBTAIN GAUGE
- Blunt-end yarn needle

PREP

gauge

12 sts and 5 rows = 4" (10 cm) over (ch-1, dc) st, with A, B, and C held tog as one. TAKE TIME TO CHECK YOUR GAUGE.

Note: To work dc around turning ch of previous row, yo, insert hook from front to back to front around turning ch, yo and draw up a lp, (yo and draw through 2 lps on hook) twice.

CROCHET

With A, B, and C held tog as one, ch 18.

Row 1: Dc in 6th ch from hook, (ch 1, sk next ch, dc in next ch) 6 times—7 ch-1 sps. Ch 2—counts as first dc of next row; turn.

Row 2: Dc in first ch-1 sp, (ch 1, dc in next ch-1 sp) 6 times, dc around turning ch of previous row (see Note above)—6 ch-1 sps. Ch 3—counts as first dc and ch-1 of next row; turn.

Row 3: Dc in first ch-1 sp, (ch 1, dc in next ch-1 sp) 5 times, ch 1, dc around turning ch of previous row—7 ch-1 sps. Ch 2; turn.

Rep Rows 2–3 until piece measures 60" or desired length from beg; fasten off. Weave in ends.

4. LAVENDER SCARF

SKILL LEVEL

Beginner

SIZE

finished measurements

7½×60"

SHOP

yarns

Brilliant from Patons (Art. 246103)
69% acrylic, 19% nylon, 12% polyester;
1¾ oz. (50 g); 166 yds. (151 m); DK weight
3 LIGHT
• 2 balls #3314 Lilac Luster (A)

Divine from Patons (Art. 241006)
79.5% acrylic, 18% mohair, 2.5% polyester;
3½ oz. (100 g); 142 yds. (129 m); bulky weight
6 SUPER BULKY
• 2 balls #6230 Lavender Mist (B)

Cha Cha from Patons (Art. 242002)
100% nylon; 1¾ oz. (50 g);
77 yds. (70 m); bulky weight
6 SUPER BULKY
• 3 balls #2117 Disco (C)

Silverlash from Patons (Art. 244081)
98% polyester, 2% lurex; 1¾ oz. (50 g);
164 yds. (150 m); worsted weight
4 MEDIUM
• 1 ball #81422 Lustrous Lilac (D)

hook & extra

- Size P/16 (11.5 mm) crochet hook OR SIZE NEEDED TO OBTAIN GAUGE
- Blunt-end yarn needle

PREP

gauge

8 sts and 4 rows = 4" (10 cm) in (ch-1, dc) st, with A, B, C, D held tog as one. TAKE TIME TO CHECK GAUGE.

Note: To work dc around turning ch of previous row, yo, insert hook from front to back to front around turning ch, yo and draw up a lp, (yo and draw through 2 lps on hook) twice.

CROCHET

With A, B, C, and D held tog as one, ch 18.

Row 1: Dc in 6th ch from hook, (ch 1, sk next ch, dc in next ch) 6 times—7 ch-1 sps. Ch 2—counts as first dc of next row; turn.

Row 2: Dc in first ch-1 sp, (ch 1, dc in next ch-1 sp) 6 times, dc around turning ch of previous row (see Note above)—6 ch-1 sps. Ch 3—counts as first dc and ch-1 of next row; turn.

Row 3: Dc in first ch-1 sp, (ch 1, dc in next ch-1 sp) 5 times, ch 1, dc around turning ch of previous row—7 ch-1 sps. Ch 2; turn. Rep Rows 2–3 until piece measures 60" from beg; fasten off. Weave in ends.

5. BLUE SCARF

SKILL LEVEL

Beginner

SIZE

finished measurements

7½×60"

SHOP

yarns

Brilliant from Patons (Art. 246103)
69% acrylic, 19% nylon, 12% polyester;
1¾ oz. (50 g); 166 yds. (151 m); DK weight
3 LIGHT
• 2 balls #3143 Blue Shimmer (A)

Divine from Patons (Art. 241006)
79.5% acrylic, 18% mohair,
2.5% polyester; 3½ oz. (100 g);
142 yds. (129 m); chunky weight
5 BULKY
• 2 balls #6106 Halo Blue (B)

Silverlash from Patons (Art. 244081)
98% polyester, 2% lurex; 1¾ oz. (50 g);
164 yds. (150 m); worsted weight
4 MEDIUM
• 1 ball #81128 Blue Brilliant (C)

Glittalic from Patons (Art. 241066)
95% polyester, 5% lurex; 1¾ oz. (50 g);
61 yds. (55m); chunky weight
5 BULKY
• 3 balls #66128 Blue Flash (D)

Lacette from Patons (Art. 243030)
39% nylon, 36% acrylic, 25% mohair;
1¾ oz. (50 g); 235 yds. (215 m); fine weight
2 FINE
• 1 ball #30128 Beautiful Blue (E)

hook & extra

- Size Q hook OR SIZE NEEDED TO OBTAIN GAUGE
- Blunt-end yarn needle

PREP

gauge

8 sts and 3 rows = 5" (12.5 cm) over (ch-1, dc) st with A, B, C, D, and E held tog as one. TAKE TIME TO CHECK YOUR GAUGE.

Note: To work dc around turning ch of previous row, yo, insert hook from front to back to front around turning ch, yo and draw up a loop, (yo and draw through 2 lps on hook) twice.

CROCHET

With A, B, C, D, and E held tog as one, ch 18.

Row 1: Dc in 6th ch from hook, (ch 1, sk next ch, dc in next ch) 6 times—7 ch-1 sps. Ch 2—counts as first dc of next row; turn.

Row 2: Dc in first ch-1 sp, (ch 1, dc in next ch-1 sp) 6 times, dc around turning ch of previous row (see Note above)—6 ch-1 sps. Ch 3—counts as first dc and ch-1 of next row; turn.

Row 3: Dc in first ch-1 sp, (ch 1, dc in next ch-1 sp) 5 times, ch 1, dc around turning ch of previous row—7 ch-1 sps. Ch 2; turn. Rep Rows 2–3 until piece measures 60" or desired length from beg; fasten off. Weave in ends.

Designs by Randy Cavalieri

zigzag élan

The shape and handle are retro; the color, ultra hot. Done in single crochet, this generous purse gets extra zip with chain-stitch stripes added afterwards.

PURPLE BAG

SKILL LEVEL

Easy

SIZE

finished measurements

13½×10×4"

SHOP

yarn

Lion Cotton from Lion Brand (Art. 760)
100% cotton; 5 oz. (140 g);
236 yds. (212 m); worsted weight
- 2 balls #147 Purple

4 MEDIUM

hooks & extras

- Size F/5 (3.75 mm) crochet hook OR SIZE NEEDED TO OBTAIN GAUGE
- Size J/10 (6 mm) crochet hook
- 11½" hinged purse frame (Lacis LD70)
- Handbag handles (#33699, color: Tartaruga)
- Fabric for lining
- Sewing needle and thread to match lining fabric
- Stitch marker
- Blunt-end yarn needle

PREP

gauge

With smaller hook, 17 sc and 17 rows = 4" (10 cm).
TAKE TIME TO CHECK YOUR GAUGE.

stitch abbreviation

Sc2tog = Draw up a loop in each of next 2 stitches, yarn over and draw through all loops on hook.

CROCHET

SIDE (make 2)

With smaller hook, ch 46.

Row 1: Sc in 2nd ch from hook and in each ch across; turn—45 sts. Place a marker on center st of this row and leave it there as a guide for finishing instructions.

Rows 2–7: Ch 1, 2 sc in first sc, sc in each sc across to last sc, 2 sc in last sc; turn—57 sts at end of Row 7.

Rows 8–10: Ch 1, sc in each sc across; turn.

Row 11: Ch 1, sc2tog, sc in each st to last 2 sts, sc2tog—55 sts; turn.

Rep last 4 rows 7 more times—41 sts.

Next 3 rows: Ch 1, sc in each sc across; turn.

Fasten off.

GUSSET

With smaller hook, ch 17.

Row 1: Sc in 2nd ch from hook and in each ch across; turn—16 sts.

Rows 2–132: Ch 1, sc in each sc across; turn.

Fasten off.

FINISHING

Work surface embellishment on the Sides as foll:
Beg at the marked st above the foundation row, with larger hook and 2 strands of yarn, work ch sts on the surface with each ch covering 2 rows and moving to the side by one sc, work 2 ch traveling to the right, *work 4 ch traveling to the left, work 4 ch traveling to the right; rep from * to top of piece; fasten off and secure the end.

Work 4 more zigzag lines of surface chs, 2 to the left and 2 to the right of the center zigzag line (sk 6 sc bet lines).

Using the Side and Gusset pieces as guides, cut the fabric lining to the same measurements, adding ½" seam allowances. Press down ½" at the top of the Sides and the ends of the Gusset. Sew the Side lining to the Gusset lining. Set the lining aside.

Attach the Gusset to one Side of the Bag with a row of sc, matching the ends of the Gusset with the top corners of the Side; ch 1, turn.

Next row: Sl st in each sc; fasten off.

Work surface embellishment on the other Side of the Bag and attach this Side to the opposite side of the Gusset in the same manner as the first Side.

Place the lining in the Bag. Attach the Bag to the frame by sandwiching the frame bet the top of the Bag and the lining.

Stitch across the top of the Bag, sewing through all thicknesses, using the holes in the frame as a guide, and leaving the Sides open.

Attach handles to the frame by wrapping yarn around the frame attachments and handle rings as shown in the photo, *opposite*.

Design by Linda Cyr

start packin'

This eminently stuffable backpack can tote anything from notebooks and pens to an iPod. Make it in a solid hue or stripe it with school colors.

DRAWSTRING TOTE

SKILL LEVEL

Easy

SIZE

finished measurements

15×13¾"

SHOP

yarns

Sugar'n Cream from Lily (Art. 102001)
100% cotton; 2½ oz. (72 g);
120 yds. (110 m); worsted weight

4 MEDIUM

- 4 balls #2 Black (A)
- 3 balls #1628 Hot Orange (B)

hook & extras

- Sizes I/9 (5.5 mm) crochet hook OR SIZE NEEDED TO OBTAIN GAUGE
- Small safety pin for marker
- Blunt-end yarn needle

PREP

gauge

12 sts and 12 rnds = 4" (10 cm) in sc with 2 strands of yarn held tog. TAKE TIME TO CHECK YOUR GAUGE.

special stitch

Join yarn with a sc = With 2 strands of yarn held together, make a slip knot and place on hook. Insert hook into stitch, yarn over and draw up a loop, yarn over and draw through 2 loops on hook.

CROCHET

With 2 strands of A held tog, ch 32.

Rnd 1 (RS): Work 2 sc in 2nd ch from hook, sc in next 29 ch, work 3 sc in last ch, do not turn; working along the opposite side of the ch, sc in next 29 ch, sc in same ch as first sc, join rnd with a sl st in first sc—64 sts.

Rnd 2: Ch 1, work 2 sc in each of first 2 sts, sc in next 29 sts, work 2 sc in each of next 3 sts, sc in next 29 sts, work 2 sc in last st, join rnd with a sl st in first sc—70 sts.

Rnd 3: Ch 1, work 2 sc in first 4 sts, sc in next 29 sts, work 2 sc in each of next 6 sts, sc in next 29 sts, work 2 sc in each of last 2 sts, do not join, mark last st made with safety pin—82 sts. You will now be working in a spiral, marking last st made with safety pin to indicate end of rnd.

Rnds 4–5: Sc in each st around.

Rnd 6: Sc in each st around, join rnd with a sl st in first st, removing safety pin; fasten off. With RS facing, join 2 strands of B with a sc in side edge opposite joining of previous rnd.

Rnd 7: Sc in each st around, do not join, mark last st made with safety pin. Now work in a spiral, marking last st made with safety pin to indicate end of rnd.

Rnds 8–11: Sc in each st around.

Rnd 12: Sc in each st around, join rnd with a sl st in first st, removing safety pin; fasten off. With RS facing, join 2 strands of A with a sc in side edge opposite joining of previous rnd.

Rnd 13: Sc in each st around, do not join, mark last st made with safety pin. Now work in a spiral, marking last st made with safety pin to indicate end of rnd.

Rnds 14–17: Sc in each st around.

Rnds 18–23: Rep Rnds 6–11.

Rnds 24–29: Rep Rnds 12–17.

Rnds 30–35: Rep Rnds 6–11.

Rnd 36: Rep Rnd 12.

Rnd 37: Sc in each st around, do not join, mark last st made with safety pin.

Rnd 38: Sc in each st around, join rnd with a sl st in first st, removing safety pin.

Rnd 39 (eyelets): Ch 4—counts as 1 dc and ch 1; sk next st, dc in next st, *ch 1, sk next st, dc in next st; rep from * around, end ch 1, sk last st, join rnd with a sl st in 3rd ch of beg ch-4.

Rnd 40 (eyelets): Ch 4—counts as 1 dc and ch 1; sk next ch-1 sp, dc in next st, *ch 1, sk next ch-1 sp, dc in next st; rep from * around, end ch 1, sk last ch-1 sp, join rnd with a sl st in 3rd ch of beg ch-4; fasten off. Weave in ends.

STRAP (make 2)

With 2 strands of A held tog, and leaving a long tail, ch 160. Fasten off, leaving a long tail.

Beg and ending at a side edge, weave the Strap through the eyelets of Rnd 39.

Thread one tail into the yarn needle. Insert the needle into the bottom corner of the Tote, drawing the end through to WS. Rep for other tail, inserting yarn needle one st away. Tie tail ends tog in a knot on the WS of the Tote. Beg and ending at the opposite side edge, weave the rem Strap through the eyelets of Rnd 40. Attach the ends to the opposite bottom corner in the same way. Adjust for length as desired.

Design by Katherine Eng

masculine manner

Treat the man in your life—Dad, brother, or "significant other"—to a handsome double-crochet scarf that reminds him of you.

CHECKERED SCARF

SKILL LEVEL

Intermediate

SIZE

finished measurements

6½×60" (excluding fringe)

SHOP

yarns

Brilla from Filatura Di Crosa

58% viscose, 42% cotton; 1¾ oz. (50 g); 120 yds. (110 m); worsted weight

- 2 balls #404 Brown (A)
- 2 balls #429 Rust (B)
- 2 balls #385 Gold (C)

hook & extra

- Size G/6 (4 mm) crochet hook OR SIZE NEEDED TO OBTAIN GAUGE
- Blunt-end yarn needle

PREP

gauge

22 sts and 8 rows = 4" (10 cm) over dc color pat with size 7 (4.5 mm) crochet hook. TAKE TIME TO CHECK YOUR GAUGE.

Notes: When changing colors, draw new color through last 2 loops on hook to complete dc.

Carry colors not in use loosely across WS of work, then work over loose strands on following row to conceal them.

Do not cut and join colors. Carry yarns loosely along side edge of work.

CROCHET

With A, ch 38.

Row 1 (RS): Dc in 4th ch from hook and in next 2 ch, change to B when working last dc; *with B, dc in next 4 ch, change to C when working 4th dc; with C, dc in next 4 ch, change to A when working 4th dc; with A, dc in next 4 ch, change to B when working 4th dc; rep from * once more; with B, dc in next 4 ch, change to C when working 4th dc; with C, dc in last 4 ch, change to B when working last dc; with B, ch 3, turn.

Note: In instructions that foll, references to changing yarn color mean you make the change when working the 4th dc of a color group.

Row 2: With B, dc in next 3 dc, change to A on last dc; *with A, dc in next 4 dc, change to C; with C, dc in next 4 dc, change to B; with B, dc in next 4 dc, change to A; rep from * once more; with A, dc in next 4 dc, change to C; with C, dc in last 3 dc and in top of turning-ch, change to B; with B, ch 3 and turn.

Row 3: With B, dc in next 3 dc, change to C; *with C, dc in next 4 dc, change to A; with A, dc in next 4 dc, change to B; with B, dc in next 4 dc, change to C; rep from * once more; with C, dc in next 4 dc, change to A; with A, dc in last 3 dc and in top of turning-ch, change to C; with C, ch 3 and turn.

Row 4: With C, dc in next 3 dc, change to B; *with B, dc in next 4 dc, change to A; with A, dc in next 4 dc, change to C; with C, dc in next 4 dc, change to B; rep from * once more; with B, dc in next 4 dc, change to A; with A, dc in last 3 dc and in top of turning-ch, change to C; with C, ch 3 and turn.

Row 5: With C, dc in next 3 dc, change to A; *with A, dc in next 4 dc, change to B; with B, dc in next 4 dc, change to C; with C, dc in next 4 dc, change to A; rep from * once more; with A, dc in next 4 dc, change to B; with B, dc in last 3 dc and in top of turning-ch, change to A; with A, ch 3 and turn.

Row 6: With A, dc in next 3 dc, change to C; *with C, dc in next 4 dc, change to B; with B, dc in next 4 dc, change to A; with A, dc in next 4 dc, change to C; rep from * once more; with C, dc in next 4 dc, change to B; with B, dc in last 3 dc and in top of turning-ch, change to A; with A, ch 3 and turn.

Row 7: With A, dc in next 3 dc, change to B; *with B, dc in next 4 dc, change to C; with C, dc in next 4 dc, change to A; with A, dc in next 4 dc, change to B; rep from * once more; with B, dc in next 4 dc, change to C; with C, dc in last 3 dc and in top of turning-ch, change to B; with B, ch 3 and turn.

Rep Rows 2–7 for 18 times, then rep Rows 2–6 one more time.

Next row: With A, dc in next 3 dc, change to B; *with B, dc in next 4 dc, change to C; with C, dc in next 4 dc, change to A; with A, dc in next 4 dc, change to B; rep from * once more; with B, dc in next 4 dc, change to C; with C, dc in last 3 dc and in top of turning-ch, change to B; with B, ch 1 and turn.

Next row: Sc in each dc across; fasten off and weave in ends.

FRINGE

Cut forty-eight 10" strands of each color.

Put 2 strands of B tog and fold in half. With WS of top edge facing, use hook to draw center of strands through first st, forming a lp. Pull ends of strands through this lp. Pull to tighten.

In this manner, make a fringe in each st along top edge, using colors to correspond to color pat. Trim the strands even if necessary.

Rep along bottom edge working in bottom lps of beg ch.

Design by Randy Cavalieri

band of blooms

Gather up a bouquet of colorful cotton thread for this fresh headband. The design consists of three rosy motifs finished with end triangles and long chain-stitch ties.

FLOWER HEADBAND

SKILL LEVEL

Intermediate

SIZE

finished measurement

8½" (excluding ties)

SHOP

threads

Senso Cotton from DMC (Art. 700U)
100% cotton; 1.52 oz. (43 g);
150 yds. (137 m); sport weight
- 1 ball #1008 Bright Pink (A)

2 FINE

Senso Microfiber Cotton from DMC (Art. 710)
60% cotton, 40% acrylic; 1.52 oz. (43 g);
150 yds. (137 m); sport weight
- 1 ball #1109 Blue (B)
- 1 ball #1108 Spring Green (C)

hook & extras

- Size F/5 (3.75 mm) crochet hook OR SIZE NEEDED TO OBTAIN GAUGE
- Blunt-end yarn needle
- Sewing thread to match thread C
- Embroidery needle

PREP

gauge

1 motif = 2" square (5 cm). TAKE TIME TO CHECK YOUR GAUGE.

CROCHET

FLOWER MOTIF (make 3; 2 with B as center and 1 with A as center)

Foundation ring: Using A (B), ch 6, join with sl st to form a ring.

Rnd 1 (RS): Ch 5—counts as dc, and ch 2; (dc in ring, ch 2) 7 times, join with sl st in 3rd ch of ch-5. Fasten off—8 dc and 8 ch-2 lps.

Rnd 2: With RS facing, join B (A) with sl st in next ch-2 sp, ch 1, in same sp work sc, hdc, 2 dc, hdc, sc—one petal made; in each ch-2 sp around work sc, hdc, 2 dc, hdc, and sc; join with sl st in first sc. Fasten off.

Rnd 3: With RS facing, join C in back lp of same sc as last sl st, ch 5; working in back lps, (sl st in first sc of next petal, ch 5) 7 times; join with sl st in first ch of ch-5.

Rnd 4: Sl st into next ch-5 sp, ch 1, 6 sc into same sp; *work 3 dc, ch 2, and 3 dc in next ch-5 sp**, 6 sc in next ch-5 sp; rep from * twice and from * to ** once again; join with sl st into first sc. Fasten off.

Alternating the flower colors, join the Flower Motifs in a strip.

END TRIANGLE (make 2)

With RS facing, join C with a sl st in a ch-2 corner at one end of strip.

Row 1: Ch 2—counts as hdc; (yo and draw up a lp in next dc) 2 times; yo and draw through all 5 lps on hook—hdc dec made; hdc in next 8 sts, hdc dec over next 2 dc; (sk ch-2 sp)—11 sts; turn.

Row 2: Ch 2—counts as hdc; sk next st, hdc dec, hdc in next 5 sts, hdc dec over next 2 sts—8 sts; turn.

Row 3: Ch 2—counts as hdc; sk next st, hdc dec over next 2 sts, hdc in next 2 st, hdc dec over next 2 sts—5 sts; turn.

Row 4: Ch 2—counts as hdc; sk next st, hdc in next 2 hdc, sk last st—3 sts; turn.

Row 5: Ch 2, sk next st, hdc in next hdc—2 sts. Do not fasten off thread.

Chain Tie (make 2)

Ch 100, sc in 2nd ch from hook and in each ch across; end with sl st in corresponding hdc of Row 5. Fasten off.

Design adapted from a block-motif by Jan Eaton

CROCHET

basics

Here's all the information you'll need: stitch instructions, abbreviations, and the lowdown on skill levels to help you select an easy project or one that will stretch your abilities.

SKILL LEVELS DEFINED

BEGINNER

Projects for first-time crocheters are labeled "Beginner." These patterns use basic stitches, minimal shaping, and very simple finishing.

EASY

Projects labeled "Easy" use basic stitches, repetitive stitch patterns, simple color changes, and simple shaping and finishing.

INTERMEDIATE

Projects labeled "Intermediate" use a variety of techniques, such as lace or color patterns, with midlevel shaping and finishing.

EXPERIENCED

Projects labeled "Experienced" use advanced techniques and stitches, with detailed shaping and refined finishing.

ABBREVIATIONS

approx approximately
beg begin(ning)(s)
bet between
BPdc back post double crochet
CC contrasting color
ch chain
ch- refers to chain or space previously made
ch-sp chain-space
cont continue
dc double crochet
dc cl double crochet cluster
dc2tog double crochet 2 stitches together
dec decrease
end ending
est established
foll follow(ing)(s)
FPdc front post double crochet
FPsc front post single crochet
FPtr front post treble crochet
hdc half double crochet
hdc2tog half double crochet 2 stitches together
inc increase
lp(s) loop(s)
MC main color
pat pattern
rem remain(ing)(s)
rep repeat
rnd(s) round(s)
RS right side
sc single crochet
sc2tog single crochet 2 stitches together
sc3tog single crochet 3 stitches together
sk skip
sl st slip stitch
sp(s) space(s)
st(s) stitch(es)
tog together
tr treble crochet
tr cl treble crochet cluster
WS wrong side
yo yarn over
[ ] work instructions within brackets as many times as directed
( ) work instructions within parentheses as many times as directed
***** repeat the instructions following the single asterisk as directed
*** *** repeat instructions between asterisks as many times as directed, or repeat from a set of instructions (sometimes you will see as many as three or four sets of asterisks; the same directions apply)
" inch(es)

STANDARD YARN WEIGHT SYSTEM

Categories of yarn, gauge ranges, and recommended hook sizes

Yarn Weight Symbol & Category Names	1 SUPER FINE	2 FINE	3 LIGHT	4 MEDIUM	5 BULKY	6 SUPER BULKY
Type of Yarns in Category	Sock, Fingering, Baby	Sport, Baby	DK, Light Worsted	Worsted, Afghan, Aran	Chunky, Craft, Rug	Bulky, Roving
Crochet Gauge* Ranges in Single Crochet to 4 inches	21–32 sts	16–20 sts	12–17 sts	11–14 sts	8–11 sts	5–9 sts
Recommended Hook in Metric Size Range	2.25 mm to 3.5 mm	3.5 mm to 4.5 mm	4.5 mm to 6.5 mm	5.5 mm to 6.5 mm	6.5 mm to 9 mm	9 mm and larger
Recommended Hook in U.S. Size Range	B/1 to E/4	E/4 to 7	7 to I/9	I/9 to K/10½	K/10½ to M/13	M/13 and larger

*GUIDELINES ONLY: The above reflect the most commonly used gauges and hook sizes for specific yarn categories.

slip knot

1. Make a loop; then hook another loop through it.

2. Tighten gently and slide the knot up to the hook.

chain stitch (ch)

1. Make a slip knot. Yarn over the hook and draw the yarn through to form a new loop without tightening up the previous one.

2. Repeat to form as many chains as required. Do not count the slip knot as a chain stitch.

single crochet (sc)

1. Insert the hook into the work (second chain from hook on the starting chain), *yarn over the hook, and draw up a loop through the work only—two loops are on the hook.

2. Yarn over the hook again and draw the yarn through both loops on the hook—one single crochet made.

3. Insert the hook into the next stitch; repeat from * in step 1.

half double crochet (hdc)

1. Yarn over the hook and insert the hook into the work (third chain from the hook on the starting chain).

2. Yarn over the hook and draw up a loop through the work only—three loops on the hook.

3. Yarn over the hook again and draw through all three loops on the hook—one half double crochet made.

4. Yarn over the hook, insert the hook into the next stitch; repeat from step 2.

double crochet (dc)

1. Yarn over the hook and insert the hook into the work (fourth chain from the hook on the starting chain).

2. Yarn over the hook and draw through the work only—three loops are on the hook.

3. Yarn over the hook and draw through the first two loops only—two loops are on the hook.

4. Yarn over the hook and draw through the last two loops on the hook—one double crochet made.

5. Yarn over the hook, insert the hook into the next stitch; repeat from step 2.

treble crochet (tr)

1. Yarn over the hook two times and insert the hook into the work (fifth chain from the hook on the starting chain).
2. Yarn over the hook and draw through the work only—four loops are on the hook.
3. Yarn over the hook and draw through the first two loops on the hook—three loops are on the hook.
4. Yarn over the hook and draw through the next two loops on the hook—two loops remain on the hook.
5. Yarn over the hook again and draw through remaining two loops on hook—one treble crochet made. Repeat steps 1–5, working a treble crochet in each chain across.

slip stitch (sl st)

This is the shortest crochet stitch and, unlike other stitches, is not used on its own to produce a fabric. It is used for joining, shaping, and where necessary, carrying the yarn to another part of the fabric for the next stage.

1. Insert the hook into the work (second chain from hook), yarn over, and draw the yarn through both the work and the loop on the hook in one movement.
2. To join chains into a ring with a slip stitch, insert the hook into the first chain, yarn over, and draw through both the work and the yarn on the hook in one movement.

chain stitch

To embroider a chain stitch, pull the needle up at A, form a U shape with the thread, and hold the shape in place with your thumb. Push the needle down at B, and come up at C. Continue in the same manner.

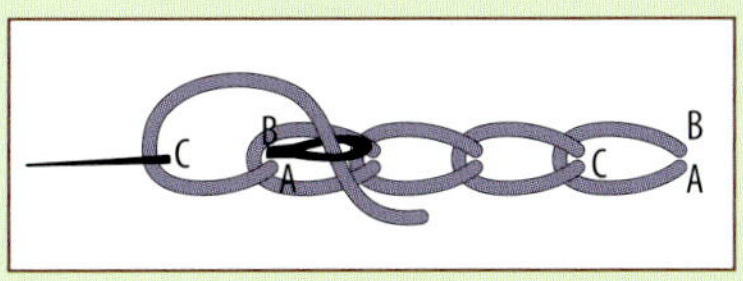

stitch abbreviations

Sc2tog = Draw up a loop in each of next 2 stitches, yarn over and draw through all loops on hook.

Sc3tog = Draw up a loop in each of next 3 stitches, yarn over and draw through all loops on hook—2-stitch decrease made.

reverse single crochet

This neat, narrow edging is perfect for finishing the edges of a crochet project. The important thing to remember is that you work this stitch from left to right instead of right to left—that's why it's called reverse single crochet. (The stitch also is referred to as backward stitch or crab stitch.)

1. Starting on the left side of the crocheted piece, pull a slip knot through the end stitch. Chain one. *Draw up a loop in the next stitch to the right. Catch the yarn with the hook and pull it through the fabric and under but not through the loop already on the hook.
2. Bring the yarn over and around the top of the hook. Draw the yarn through both loops on the hook. Repeat from * in step 1.

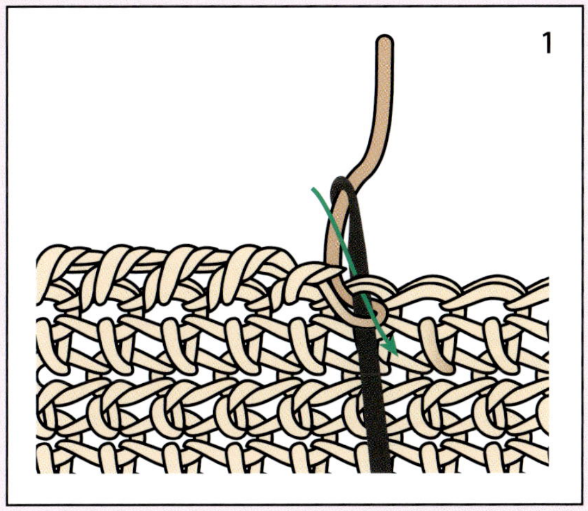

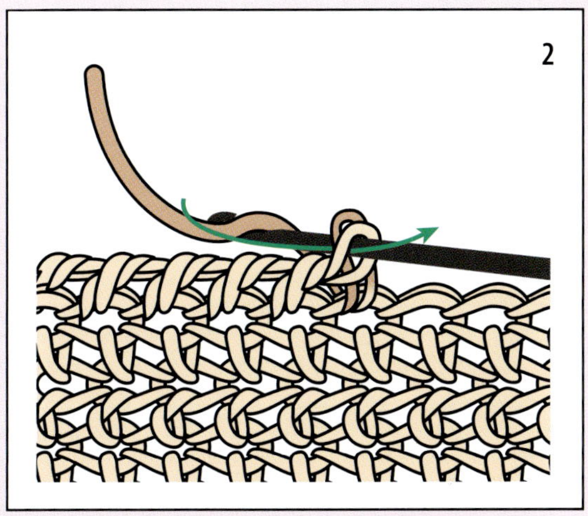

Better Homes and Gardens® Creative Collection®

Editorial Director John Riha

Editor in Chief Deborah Gore Ohrn

Executive Editor Karman Wittry Hotchkiss

Managing Editor Kathleen Armentrout

Contributing Editorial Manager Heidi Palkovic

Contributing Design Director Tracy DeVenney

Contributing Editor Laura Holtorf Collins
Contributing Designer Carrie Naumann
Copy Chief Mary Heaton
Contributing Copy Editor Jennifer Horejsi
Proofreader Joleen Ross
Administrative Assistant Lori Eggers

Publishing Group President
Jack Griffin

Meredith CORPORATION

President and CEO Stephen M. Lacy

Chairman of the Board William T. Kerr

In Memoriam
E. T. Meredith III (1933–2003)